Michel de C

Theory, Culture & Society

Theory, Culture & Society caters for the resurgence of interest in culture within contemporary social science and the humanities. Building on the heritage of classical social theory, the book series examines ways in which this tradition has been reshaped by a new generation of theorists. It also publishes theoretically informed analyses of everyday life, popular culture, and new intellectual movements.

EDITOR: Mike Featherstone, *Nottingham Trent University*

THE TCS CENTRE
The Theory, Culture & Society book series, the journals *Theory, Culture & Society* and *Body & Society*, and related conference, seminar and postgraduate programmes operate from the TCS Centre at Nottingham Trent University. For further details of the TCS Centre's activities please contact:

Centre Administrator
The TCS Centre, Room 175
Faculty of Humanities
Nottingham Trent University
Clifton Lane, Nottingham, NG11 8NS, UK
e-mail: tcs@ntu.ac.uk
web: http://tcs@ntu.ac.uk

Recent volumes include:

Feminist Imagination
Vikki Bell

The Cultural Economy of Cities
Allen J. Scott

Body Modification
edited by Mike Featherstone

Paul Virilio
edited by John Armitage

Michel de Certeau

Cultural Theorist

Ian Buchanan

SAGE Publications
London • Thousand Oaks • New Delhi

First published 2000

Published in association with *Theory, Culture & Society*, Nottingham Trent University

SAGE Publications Ltd
6 Bonhill Street
London EC2A 4PU

SAGE Publications Inc
2455 Teller Road
Thousand Oaks, California 91320

SAGE Publications India Pvt Ltd
32, M-Block Market
Greater Kailash - I
New Delhi 110 048

British Library Cataloguing in Publication data

A catalogue record for this book is available from the British Library.

ISBN 0 7619 587 5
ISBN 0 7619 5898 3 pbk

Library of Congress catalog card record available

Printed in Great Britain by Athenaeum Press, Gateshead

For Horst Ruthrof

Contents

Acknowledgements

I must first of all thank Chris Rojek for commissioning this volume. Besides the confidence it displayed in me, it confirmed my view that de Certeau is an important thinker whose time is now. I must also thank several of my fellow travellers in the field of de Certeau studies: Tom Conley has been an unflagging ally for several years now and I couldn't have written this book without his support; Michael B. Smith has been extremely generous with his time and work (commenting on drafts of this and other pieces as well as giving me access to his forthcoming translation of *The Possession of Loudun*); Richard Terdiman has been my conscience: under his watchful eye many simplifications and bad reductions have been avoided (those that remain are entirely my fault); Jeremy Ahearne has been an extremely important correspondent (our dialogues have, for me at least, always been helpful and productive); Roland Boer, Graham Ward and Fritz Bauerschmidt have opened my eyes to a dimension of de Certeau's thought I would otherwise not have seen (literally they have been 'spirit guides'); special thanks, too, must go to Claire Colebrook, a true friend and colleague. Finally, I must thank my wife, Tanya Buchanan, for enduring my decade long obsession with de Certeau's work.

Ian Buchanan
Hobart, Tasmania.
February 2000

Introduction

> Speculation and calculation induce us to move beyond the world of
> sensible reality; they reveal to us that this world is bounded by enabling
> us to look at its boundaries from the outside.
>
> Georg Simmel, *On Individuality and Social Forms*

Born in 1925 in Chambéry, de Certeau did not study theology straight
away, nor enter the order that was to become his life immediately upon
attaining majority; rather he first of all obtained degrees in classics and
philosophy at the universities of Grenoble, Lyon and Paris.[1] He didn't in
fact enter the Jesuits until 1950, and wasn't ordained until 1956 (it is
said he joined the Jesuits in the hope of working in China, but alas
world events conspired against him and China turned out to be one of
the few places he did not travel to).[2] He completed a doctorate in
theology at the Sorbonne in 1960, his thesis topic was the mystical
writings of Jean-Joseph Surin. As is so often the case with one's
doctoral research, his interest in Surin's writing was lifelong; he was to
return to it several times after both the dissertation and the enormously
laborious scholarly editions of Surin's work he prepared following it
were published.

What makes de Certeau's beginnings so interesting is the fact that
they do not seem to have prepared him in any direct way for the future
paths he would take. It is now legend that in 1968, when the streets of
Paris erupted in a paroxysm of student, then blue-collar, protest that de
Certeau underwent some kind of personal transformation – a shattering,
he called it. Much of this legend stems from the fact that de Certeau was
able to capture the essence of the events with his on the spot theorising,
which he initially published as a series of short articles in the Catholic
monthly *Études*, and reprinted in book form with slight revisions in *La
prise de parole* (*The Capture of Speech*) which first appeared in
October of the same year. What made his accounts so unusual, giving
him instant, but lasting fame (unlike many others who similarly shot to
prominence in this turbulent period then vanished from public view
almost as swiftly) was their even-handedness: de Certeau was alert to
the potentiality of the events, but wise to the reality.

Practically, he saw, nothing changed, but politically everything had changed – the old regime no longer had the authority it had once commanded; consequently it could no longer hold fast against further changes. De Certeau's next career move follows on logically from this insight: an opportunity was put before him in the form of a large research grant to study culture on a broad scale and investigate more fully just how much things had changed in recent times, if at all. The main emphasis of the project was meant to be futurology as far as the granting body (DGRST) was concerned, but de Certeau had little taste for it and in the final writing up of the research it was downplayed (Giard, 1998a: xviii). The legacy of this work is the two volumes of the *Practice of Everyday Life*. Of a similar order, though prepared under different circumstances, but still government funded (the OECD this time), is the work on migrants found now in *Culture in the Plural*.

While it is undoubtedly true that in English-speaking circles it is to this work from the middle period of his career that de Certeau owes his fame, it should not be thought that they somehow eclipse his other work in either importance or interest. The work de Certeau did before and after this, which covers a range of topics that can be loosely placed together under the heading of historiography, is equally noteworthy. And though it is well known in cultural studies it seems to be read only for its topical interest, as it were, the fact that it touches on such exotic subjects as cannibalism, seventeenth-century travel writing, the origins of anthropology and so on, but not, sadly, its methodology, which in these post-structuralist times perhaps feels a little passé. The marked influence of Greimas and Marin on this work is yet to be fully assessed, but sometimes it feels as if it has already been dismissed. The fact that his meta-historiography tends to be approached from the perspective of two vastly more influential figures, namely Lacan and Foucault, probably explains this blind spot in secondary writing on de Certeau.

Much of the cachet de Certeau's work now enjoys in Anglo-American cultural studies is attributable to the very select way it has been disseminated in English. Thanks to the enormous success of *The Practice of Everyday Life* (with sales now in excess of 25 000 copies it is a veritable best-seller), concepts like 'strategy' and 'tactics' have been let become unruly orphans, while de Certeau's unwavering religiosity, which is nowhere absent in his work, has been quietly dropped from view altogether. With precisely these kinds of distortions, or weak misreadings as we might also choose to call them, in mind, this book is designed to be a concerted intervention into the Anglo-American 'reception' of de Certeau's work rather than an exhaustive explication of his work. I begin, here, with what is perhaps the most basic aspect of that process of reception: its translation, editing and publication; in short, its dissemination. My purpose is not to point the finger at any one in particular, and certainly not at the translators involved, but rather to point up the presence of a lasting problematic de Certeau has left us with, namely the obstacle posed to genuine plurality by alterity.

Of course, no one can be blamed for the unbalanced fame of one book. It is just one of those things that happen without anybody really being responsible. Having said that, it also needs to be acknowledged that the disproportionate success of *The Practice of Everyday Life* has not only cast a shadow over everything else that de Certeau has written, such that it is read either in exclusion of the rest of the oeuvre or as its hermeneutic keystone, it has also lately begun to dictate which of his other works will be translated, and what's more interesting, started to impact on the editorial process as well. For instance, Tom Conley (2000) informs us that it was the University of Minnesota Press's market research into the sales of *The Practice of Everyday Life* which fostered the translations of volume two of *The Practice of Everyday Life* as well as *The Capture of Speech* and *Culture in the Plural*, all of which they presented as 'companion volumes'. The problem, as I see it, is that this process of marketing de Certeau runs counter to his most deeply held convictions. According to de Certeau's view of things, readers insinuate themselves into texts in the same way that renters make habitable another's space (1984: xx–xxi), therefore any editorial process thwarting this would have to be seen as contrary to the spirit of his work, if not the letter.

Now, in a market economy, the 'companion volume' strategy no doubt makes good commercial sense, but from the perspective of understanding an author's life work it raises issues that academic publishers seem not to want to deal with anymore. However welcome the publication of these three books is, it must also be regretted that on the evidence of the way they have been marketed it is beginning to seem that only those books which thanks to a continuity of content can ride on the coat-tails of *The Practice of Everyday Life* will be translated. One can only hope that this fear will prove groundless. And while there is some reason to be hopeful, in view of the fact that The University of Chicago Press are publishing *The Possession of Loudun*, an experiment in historiographic writing which bears scant resemblance to *The Practice of Everyday Life*, there is still a bias in favour of the more secular works (indeed, none of the explicitly religious works have been translated) that needs to be corrected if a balanced view is ever to be attained among Anglophone readers.

The three most recent translations of de Certeau's work into English are additionally interesting for the way at an editorial level they seem to 'shepherd' his work. So diligent is the editorial work it borders on what I would call – playing on the Freudian notion of 'over-determination' – 'over-editing'. This process, it seems to me, is in need of interrogation because lately it has come to feel like so much spin-doctoring, though I'm quite sure it is not so cynical as that. In this respect, I find Luce

Giard's updating of de Certeau's work through the addition of a battery of editorial notes especially troubling. The notes fall into three different categories, and in general one would say they are intended only to be helpful, but that doesn't mean they don't also introduce a tendential movement into de Certeau's work at the level of the substrate which carries the unwary reader off in a direction they didn't choose. The first type of note, one which is common to all translations, might be classified simply as the background note. The second type, which is also a standard type of note, especially in critical editions, is the cross-reference, which situates the present work in the context of the author's oeuvre as a whole. The third type is not a traditional one, and no ready description of it is at hand. Its basic characteristic though is anachronism.

Editorial notes, as every text editor and translator knows, are always a double-edged sword. In some cases the supply of historical, but even more importantly, geographical and/or linguistic, background information relevant to a certain section of text is going to be absolutely crucial to its being understood by a certain type of reader. This is clearly true of the explanatory notes Tom Conley provides in his capacity as translator, giving us the historical reference to de Certeau's use of the term Fachoda for instance, but whether it is true of the anecdotal disclosures Luce Giard in her role as editor adds to *The Capture of Speech* concerning May 1968 is less certain. The problem is they are *her* anecdotes, not de Certeau's, which despite the unassailable authority they have owing to the fact of her actually having been there, all those years ago, ultimately means they are utterly heterogeneous to de Certeau's text. In many ways, these notes feel like the marginalia an interested and enthusiastic reader might scribble alongside the published text, signalling their agreement by noting the personal sparks it sets off, but their effect is nowhere near as innocent.

When such notes are actually inscribed *in* the text, they have the effect of creating a luminous 'one who knows': a preferred reader standing in the place of the implied author, displacing the implied reader altogether and thereby absorbing what limited freedom the casual reader once had. Giard's anecdotes become straitjackets to the reader who would try to follow in her footsteps. So, far from opening the text up to the unfamiliar reader as the background note is supposed to, Giard's notes tend to shut the text down. Because they go beyond the traditional parameters of their formal purpose of supplying additional information and act as a model and precedent for a type of reading the late-comer to de Certeau's works knows he or she can never hope to reproduce, unless they have a time-machine, they introduce a powerful strain of forclusion the reader is helpless against. Compared to this, the cross-reference type of note might not seem to present much of a problem. After all, isn't its purpose simply to assist the interested reader to locate related material by the same author? Yet, when one puts it like this, it also becomes clear that it poses the same problem as the first type of note, though in a slightly different way.

Whereas the anecdotal note foregrounds an 'other' reader in a way one cannot ignore, the cross-reference hides that other reader behind a screen of objectivity called 'editing'. One is often thankful to the editor for their notes, for the way they connect one text to another creating a helpful user's map. By the same token though, pointing out, for example, that de Certeau writes about mysticism in a number of different places (which all bear examination), also amounts to dictating to the reader which topic should be given weight. In other words, the cross-reference implies preference, it is a subtle (because its form has become naturalised) means of introducing predetermination into the way an oeuvre is tackled ('now you've read this, really you should read that and it'd be a pity if you didn't take a peek at such and such as well'). It creates a hierarchy, or a tree, as the Deleuzian in me is tempted to put it, where there ought to be a rhizome. Instead of the reader being able to make any connection they feel like, from any point within the text to any point within any other text, the cross-reference instructs the reader to make this moment in the text connect with this other moment in another text. Insidiously, it asserts a whole without ever bringing it into view (in this respect, as I will explain more fully in Chapter 4, it is precisely heterological in de Certeau's sense of the word).

As such it creates its own more or less private laminar flow, to use another of Deleuze's analogies, that takes the reader along a rigorously determined path. The same should probably be said of the third type of editorial intervention mentioned above, what I have called the anachronistic note. But while the previous two types of note have their precedents within the tradition of textual editing, where their respective merits and problems have been extensively debated already – I have only skimmed the surface of this scholarly discussion, much of which, I hasten to add, is technical without necessarily being theoretical in design or intent – the same cannot be said for the anachronistic note. Here I have in mind such startling interpolations as the one Giard appends to Chapter 12 of *The Capture of Speech* announcing that the 'success of Steven Spielberg's *Jurassic Park* (1993) and the attraction of historical fictions staged by Euro-Disney' convey the same themes as the original examples – an interest in astronomy and/or evolutionary biology – do, namely a desire to imbue the cosmos with meaning. Now, given that this chapter stems from a piece jointly written by Giard and de Certeau the right of one of its authors to update the text seems indisputable. And of course it is, but that isn't the issue.

Rather, what is at stake is the effect of such an anachronism as a reference to a film which appeared several years after de Certeau's death. First of all, through being yet another example of the marginalia type of personal note it reinforces the sense intuited above that the text is somehow, already definitively read. Beyond that, though, it gives the original text a predictive value it would otherwise be up to the reader to assess for themselves. It plays on its own, internalised 'critical distance', that is, the gap between its first publication and its subsequent appearance, using it to make the first version seem prophetic by virtue of the latter day examples which can be added thanks to its reissue. Here the alien quality of the note is actually a key to its success; its effect depends on it being understood as belonging to another, more recent time, thus it is assiduously signalled as such. Even aside from the peculiar difficulties posed by these problematically 'personal' notes, any historical note added to a text so 'of the moment' as *The Capture of Speech* is going to raise problems of the type Derrida catalogued under the rubric of the 'supplement' – the addition they make is simultaneously a subtraction. What it gives with one hand it takes away with the other.

Knowing that Paris was a rumour mill 'that May' helps us keep the disparate stories de Certeau juggles in perspective; it also restores some of the vivacity of the times by reminding us how tumultuous it was back then. Yet that is also the very problem: what made de Certeau's account of May 1968 so important was its very freshness, its close proximity to the times, the unmatched feeling that the author was in the swim of things and an editor's note, which besides the information it gives also functions as a figuration of time and distance itself, cannot but disrupt this. In Benjamin's terms (1968: 74), there is a contradiction at the level of their mode of intention, even though their respective objects of intention are in fact complementary: the historical note reminds us of a previously revolutionary time, but does not itself issue from that time. It is true that within de Certeau's own work – I am thinking particularly of *The Possession of Loudun* – there is a precedent for such a static dialectic of past and present placed alongside one another, but that doesn't change the fact that *The Capture of Speech* is a much altered text. It is no longer 'of the moment' in the way it was when first published, nor could it be, yet just what its 'place' is now, isn't clear either. Is it a relic?

The suspicion that twenty years after the event the exciting proximity of *The Capture of Speech* to its times will have become the single most interesting aspect of the text, making it more a curio than a work of critical historiography perhaps explains the way it has been augmented by the addition of 'other political writings' for both its 1994 republication in French and its 1997 translation into English. Confirming this view, perhaps, is Giard's positioning of de Certeau's text as an historical exhibit, all but admitting it has no predictive value, nor continuing critical valency (something both the translator Tom

Conley and blurb writer Richard Terdiman disagree with). Thus, in her introduction to *The Capture of Speech* Giard writes: 'In these pages by Michel de Certeau, the reader will discover penetrating analyses, illuminating intuitions, ideas and concepts, new information, and new perspectives. Most valuable, because it is extremely rare, is the chance to watch the work of a powerful and generous intelligence' (1997a: xix). In contrast, Conley sees the point of the translation as being an active displacement of de Certeau's thinking into the present.

What this displacement does, by foregrounding the formal aspects of de Certeau's method – its form – rather than the specific historical content of his commentaries, is make the analyses of that mythic moment fresh all over again.[3] By setting aside the merely historical in such a way as to let the method speak for itself, and speak against the content if need be, Conley's afterword depicts a very different de Certeau to the one Giard's introduction provides. Whereas for Giard it is an author in aspic, for Conley it is a very lively text demanding serious attention still. 'It is tempting' Conley writes, 'to say that the idea behind the English re-edition of Michel de Certeau's essays on the revolt of 1968 and their aftermath has been conceived, on a minor scale, to promulgate an event of a similar order. The essays in this volume cry out for consciousness. In this respect, their sheer poetic and analytic force, no matter what may be their anachronism, constitutes a timely impetus for action' (1997: 176). It may well be the tension between the introduction and the afterword that goes furthest towards the provoking of this consciousness Conley is calling for, because the editorial process has resulted in de Certeau's work being situated on an extremely 'contradictory' platform in the classical dialectic sense of the word.

I often wonder what de Certeau – who was himself fascinated by the marvellous evolution texts undergo at the hands of editors and publishers and clearly took keen delight in the effect that translation had on his work – would make of the fate of his texts.[4] Interestingly, though not I believe instructively, he left them in the safe-keeping of the very one (Luce Giard) who is responsible for the bulk of the problematic transformations surveyed above.[5] In his own lifetime, he so marvelled at the transformation of his French into English that he was moved to declaim: 'the art of translation smuggles in a thousand inventions which, before the author's dazzled eyes, transform his book into a new creation' (de Certeau, 1984: x). This note, placed at the beginning of *The Practice of Everyday Life*, suggests that de Certeau was excited by the lively and almost autonomous inner creativity with which translators are able to imbue another's text. Yet I have also heard that he was rather precious where his work was concerned. Certainly there are signs he was exacting. Both *The Practice of Everyday Life* and *Heterologies* were revised by his direction, although in the latter instance the revisions were actually carried out by Luce Giard. Both bear the signs of this.

Perhaps because he was still working on it when he moved to California in 1978 to take up a teaching post in San Diego, *The Practice of Everyday Life* was the first full length work of de Certeau's to be translated into English. Sadly, it was the only translation he was able to supervise in full himself. One important consequence, though, of his close attention to this process was the reworking of its title, which, by rights, perhaps should have been something like *The Invention of Everyday Life*, or maybe even *The Inventiveness of the Everyday*. Perversely, though, the shift from *L'invention du quotidien* to *The Practice of Everyday Life* did not result in an added emphasis being placed on the creativity of everyday life as de Certeau is reported to have wanted. On the contrary, I would say it has resulted in a hardening of 'practices' into quasi-objects.[6] A similar kind of rear-view mirror effect took place following the naming of the second of de Certeau's books to be translated into English *Heterologies*. Its title reflects an anticipated but never completed project that de Certeau had it in mind to do one day on the anthropology of belief (which I discuss in more detail in Chapter 4). He did not live to elaborate the doctrine to which the term 'heterology' is now applied in his name.

In other words, the best of intentions, including the author's own, do not always have the effects they intend – new titles can refract a text in a way impossible to anticipate, and the addition of a few editor's notes here and there can completely transform a text. All of this is exacerbated by the vagaries of translation. It is further complicated by the fact that the original text, the one that we might look to for answers here, is itself a myth. There is no 'other' pristine text which has been tarnished by the many hands involved in editing, translating and published; there is only that which is before us. This is not to say that these things do not matter, in the end, for patently they do, but to stress they are just some among many questions that must be raised. If I have chosen to begin with this set of questions it is because they seem to me at once the most elemental and perhaps for that very reason also the least asked. As de Certeau would surely have said, any thoroughgoing critique – in the most positive sense of that term – should begin at the beginning, finding that which is overlooked because it has merged with the surface itself. That, at least, is the watchword for this book that I have taken from de Certeau.

Someone once said to me, in a way I think they presumed would be insulting, that 'my' de Certeau was unrecognisable to them. That, I replied, was my point. My aim here is to defamiliarise de Certeau, as such this book is designed not so much to introduce de Certeau to unfamiliar readers as provoke a re-reading of his work among new and existing readers alike at a time when, all too soon, for some at least, de

Certeau's contribution to cultural studies is starting to seem 'historical' in the bad sense of being out of date.[7] I have thus not tried to be comprehensive, but on the contrary, pointedly selective: I have concentrated on those aspects of his work that appeared in most urgent need of some kind of estrangement. I should add, too, that the 'theological' de Certeau and the deeply 'French' de Certeau remain inaccessible to me for obvious reasons of background and disposition and I have not tried to tackle these aspects of his work, save to point out the necessity of factoring them into the equation. This doesn't mean I have ignored either his religiosity or his historical situation; but since I am neither French nor a theologian it does mean I am in no position to evaluate either of these elements of de Certeau's work. I cannot say if his brand of theological reasoning is sound or not, nor can I say which aspects of his thought are purely situational.

My position, though, is that a fallback onto biography is no solution – far better to go forward via an interrogation of concepts. Thus, rather than a set of correctives, what I offer is something I hope is more constructive: a change of perspective. The adoption of different points of view is my basic means of defamiliarising de Certeau's thought. So I begin by trying to reconstruct his plane of immanence, a Deleuzian notion, and follow it up with a Benjaminesque interrogation of his style. I then use Greimas – in a decidedly Jamesonian way, to be sure – to come at two of de Certeau's most notorious concepts, strategy and tactics, in a fresh and one hopes refreshing way. And at the end, I excavate de Certeau's crucial theoretical debts and allegiances to Merleau-Ponty and Lacan in order to make more explicit his theory of space.

Notes

[1] All biographical information is drawn from Giard, 1991a; 1991b; 1997a; 1997b; 1998a; 1998b.

[2] De Certeau's propensity for travel is recorded by a number of his erstwhile colleagues, see Chartier, 1997; Moignt, 1996; Giard, 1991a; Hartog, 1987.

[3] The influence of Benjamin is unmistakable here: 'The task of the translator consists in finding that intended effect [*Intention*] upon the language into which he is translating which produces in it the echo of the original' (1968: 76).

[4] Nowhere is de Certeau's fascination for the evolution of texts more obviously displayed than in his astonishingly erudite mapping of the fate of a certain letter written by Jean-Joseph Surin (1630) concerning a conversation with a young man in a coach (de Certeau, 1992: 206–40).

[5] Luce Giard is de Certeau's literary executor.

[6] On this last point it is perhaps worth noting that the final French title is not the original or – 'working' – choice either. There seems to have been some important shifts in thinking on this score too because in an article

published prior to the book itself, its pre-publication title is given as *Pratiques quotidiennes. Pour une sémiotique de la culture ordinaire* (de Certeau, 1980a: 3n3).

[7] Critics like Morris (1990) and Morse (1990) have already pronounced his anachronism.

1. The Plane of Immanence

> A beginning must be found which is not yet the presentation of an
> intelligible phenomenon, but which is rather simply a special kind of
> awakened attention on our part.
>
> Fredric Jameson, *Sartre: The Origins of a Style*

The humbling breadth of de Certeau's erudition taunts readers of his
work into making unwarranted reductions – in the hope of making it
manageable, no doubt. Specified either by period, giving us a specious
early and late de Certeau, which holds that his early work as religious
historian did not prepare him for his later career as cultural theorist, or
biography, giving us an even more specious distinction between a
religious and a secular de Certeau, as though to say in ceasing to focus
on theological issues he somehow gave up his beliefs, de Certeau's
oeuvre has been carved up and repackaged several times over, and
usually by the most well meaning of critics. Against an ideal model
that, in Deleuze's words (1995), takes an author as a whole, de
Certeau's work has been fragmented quite literally as well thanks to the
curious order in which it was translated and its subsequently rather odd
dissemination.[1] As it happens, the first translations to appear were not
the first ones noticed by cultural studies; in fact, these early translations
remain largely ignored (for example de Certeau, 1964; 1966; 1970a;
1970b; 1971). Because they appeared in the rather closed field of
religious studies journals, these earlier pieces have been passed over in
favour of the later more secular-seeming work.[2]

The key issue prompting all this intellectual prestidigitation is, I will
argue, de Certeau's religiosity. It is like a thorn in the side of strictly
secular critics; they want to use his insights and methods but don't
know how to handle his religious conviction so they suppress it. This is
easy enough to do because for the most part de Certeau's remarks on
religious topics are oriented either by historical concerns – what was the
place of the mystics in seventeenth-century France? – or anthropological
ones – what does it mean to believe? – which are readily assimilable by
non-religious critical concerns. And since these secular-looking
investigations were published in the latter part of de Certeau's career a
convenient quarantining of the thornier aspects of his thought can

comfortably and plausibly be made on the basis of biography. In this respect, de Certeau has been somewhat a victim of his own success – the greater the popularity of the later works the greater the desire to suppress the earlier ones. From the outset, de Certeau has only ever been read in an instrumental way. Yet, I would also argue, it is precisely because of the narrow and instrumental way de Certeau's work has been apprehended, by Anglophones at least, that it has been the success that it is.

For instance, Jeremy Ahearne commences his study of de Certeau by positing a '"founding rupture" (*rupture instauratice*)' in de Certeau's career that consigns everything published 'before' 1970 to the status of 'other', and though he is careful to acknowledge that these prior works may have prefigured this '"shattering" (*éclatement*)' or watershed he does not dwell on the relationship between the two periods save to suggest that the later work is haunted by the earlier (1995: 5).[3] Here, though, beneath this purely organisational manoeuvre, we encounter an even more insidious strategy of containment that licenses the admitted arbitrariness of the selection by claiming that the oeuvre itself was, in its own way, arbitrary too.[4] According to Ahearne, de Certeau 'was not interested in producing a systematic edifice, nor did he set himself up as the guardian of an erudite preserve' (1995: 3). Whether or not de Certeau's work was 'conceived as an ongoing response to a series of appeals and solicitations addressed to him directly or indirectly by others' (1995: 3) as Ahearne claims, thus making it seem an almost ad hoc adventure, is of only secondary concern, because what must really be addressed is whether or not de Certeau's presuppositions were similarly fluid. My point is that denying the existence of an overarching thesis spanning the entirety of a career, to the extreme even of ignoring a consistency of method and a durability of epistemological substrate, is really just another way of avoiding the issue of de Certeau's religiosity.

It is not just a matter of an accurate reading of de Certeau's work that is at stake here. Also at issue is the relative value of his contribution to cultural studies. If one follows Jameson, as I do, in thinking that the absence of a determinate project is a fault amounting to a complicity with the very state of affairs that critics in our time ought to be denouncing as loudly and thoroughly as possible, then the issue of de Certeau's religiosity takes on a whole new meaning. For as we shall see in the next chapter, de Certeau goes to great lengths to avoid or otherwise thwart the construction of anything smacking at all of being a 'master narrative' of the type endorsed by Jameson.

> The system has always understood that ideas and analysis, along with intellectuals who practice them, are its enemies and has evolved various ways of dealing with the situation, most notably – in the academic world – by railing against what it likes to call grand theory or master narratives at the same time that it fosters more comfortable and local

positivisms and empiricisms in the various disciplines. If you attack the concept of totality, for example, you are less likely to confront embarrassing models and analyses of that totality called late capitalism or capitalist globalisation; if you promote the local and the empirical, you are less likely to have to deal with the abstractions of class or value, without which the system cannot be understood. (Jameson, 1999: 267)

And insofar as de Certeau can be seen to promulgate a system of analysis focusing on precisely those 'local positivisms and empiricisms' that, in Jameson's view, are the hallmark of our age's anti-intellectualism, his position is exceedingly suspect from a Marxist point of view. Sadly, it seems that in cultural studies today it is precisely the misperception of him as an 'ideology free' skirmisher that actually accounts for a good part of de Certeau's rising cachet. Unfortunately, it has been de Certeau's fate, thanks largely to his persuasive and ultimately career-making (in Anglo-American circles anyway) elaboration of one such local positivism, namely his concept of tactics, to be seen as an invaluable ally in this disturbing shift towards the empty and unashamedly anti-theoretical position which, on the evidence of some of the recent uptakes of his work, cultural studies seems to want to occupy.

Yet, while it is true that de Certeau was in fact one of the more perspicacious critics of that form of generalisation Jameson calls totality and did indeed counter totalising gestures with his own brand of localising demystification, he was not, for all that, anti-theoretical, much less anti-intellectual. His most important demystifying weapon was doubtless the already mentioned notion of tactics, which, as I will try to show here, is neither anti-theoretical nor anti-intellectual in design or intention. Despite all the affirmations de Certeau generates from them, tactics are in fact his 'negative'. Now, this is not to say that I think Jameson is wrong in his assessment of the ideological implications of the present rise in volume and valency of 'local positivisms and empiricisms' because it is perfectly clear that 'if you promote the local and the empirical, you are less likely to have to deal with the abstractions of class or value' without which the system of capitalism itself cannot be understood. Time and again, one sees that a pointed focus on the local is not only an alternative to a focus on the global or systemic, it is also a means of avoiding ever having to look at the larger picture. Such a tack, obviously enough, is at least as much ideologically motivated as it is theoretically driven; because while it is true that any half-way competent 'adept' of deconstruction, for instance, can demolish a totality with childish ease, their desire to do so is not so readily explained.

It would be a hollow exercise indeed if the only reason one deconstructed a totality was because one could, or more banally still, because it was there. It is more likely that a certain theoretical ability is

preceded by a certain theoretical desire. Thus, after the manner of
Lyotard (1993), it may be useful to refer to a 'desire called the local'
when speaking of present anti-totalisation trends in cultural studies
because the theoretical marginalisation it enacts is surely ideological in
origin. A reality that is sometimes obscured by the fact that the bitterest
opponents of totalisation claim to endorse the same doctrine as its
proponents.[5] The key question is of course whether or not de Certeau
shares this 'desire called the local'? The short answer is no; the longer
answer is that what positive things de Certeau did have to say about the
local were predicated by the very important caveat that the tactical is
what people are reduced to when they are deprived of power (de
Certeau, 1984: 38). By the same token, de Certeau did not refuse
abstraction, as tends to be the case with most advocates of the local and
empirical. On the contrary, his notion of tactics is a formalisation and,
as it were, a raising up, of what would otherwise be merely local. The
more interesting answer, though, is that de Certeau used a very similar
means of meta-critique himself to the one deployed here, only he didn't
use the term desire as such.

De Certeau's discussion of the 'practices' of everyday life – under
which rubric he included the technical operations of historians,
psychoanalysts, anthropologists, and so on – did not stop at desire, an
exceedingly contemporary notion, but reached for something more
primeval still:

> Perhaps these practices correspond to an ageless art which has not only
> persisted through the institutions of successive political orders but goes
> back much further than our histories and forms strange alliances
> preceding the frontiers of humanity. These practices present in fact a
> curious analogy, and a sort of immemorial link, to the simulations,
> tricks, and disguises that certain fishes or plants execute with
> extraordinary virtuosity'. (de Certeau, 1984: 40)

The immediate aim of this wild-seeming speculation is, as he goes on to
explain, to free cultural analysis from its obsession with repressive
hypotheses. Whereas Foucault (1978) repudiated the notion of
repression with a dreamwork-like transformation of it into its opposite,
making the exercise of power productive not repressive (so that no one
can ever be fully repressed), de Certeau's way is to proclaim a multi-
millennial obstinacy, a perdurability of the practices of the weak proven
by their continued existence since the dawn of time.

Its deeper aim, though, is to provide an 'imaginary landscape', as de
Certeau puts it; something that, after Deleuze (1994), I would call the
precondition of a 'plane of immanence', or, perhaps better still, after
Bakhtin (1981), a 'chronotope', since what is fundamentally at stake
here is in fact the elaboration of a time–space continuum on which to
construct a new and indeed renewing image of culture and society. The

'imaginary landscape' 'restores what was earlier called "popular culture", but it does so in order to transform what was represented as a matrix-force of history into a mobile infinity of tactics. It thus keeps before our eyes the structure of a social imagination in which the problem constantly takes different forms and begins anew' (de Certeau, 1984: 41). This *long durée* conception of the social as a stylised coalition of basically primordial practices has the added advantage, de Certeau suggests, of thwarting 'the effects of an analysis which necessarily grasps these practices only on the margins of a technical apparatus, at the point where they alter or defeat its instruments' (1984: 41). It does this by making 'practices' in their immemorial, pre-consciousness form the basis of all procedures, whether mundane and quotidian, bureaucratic, or even technocratic, in nature.

> The procedures of this art can be found in the farthest reaches of the domain of the living, as if they managed to surmount not only the strategic distribution of historical institutions but also the break established by the very institution of consciousness. They maintain formal continuities and the permanence of a memory without language, from the depths of the ocean to the streets of our great cities. (de Certeau, 1984: 40)

Tactics, then, are not local positivisms or simple empiricisms, at all, but rather the precondition of de Certeau's plane of immanence. In fact, I would go so far as to suggest that the notion of 'tactics' (as well as its cognate 'practices') has the same function in de Certeau's work as 'desire' does in Deleuze and Guattari's: it posits a flux in which all the old categories and ideas social inquiry in any of its modes – history, sociology, anthropology, psychology, and so on – still clings to, can be dissolved. Its primary function should thus be seen as 'negative' in precisely the dialectical sense Jameson (1999) fears is rapidly being lost to us as totalising methods fall into disrepute and disuse. Effectively, de Certeau uses 'tactics' to rewire cultural analysis according to an immanently conceived grid, instead of a transcendental one, which is of course what Deleuze and Guattari employ desire to do, the main difference between the two being de Certeau's religiosity which, as I will explain in more detail below, demands he postulate at least one transcendental term, namely God. Of course, totalisation itself is by no means immune to the corrosive powers of this flux, it too must suffer redefinition and retooling. Its new form is that of the plane of immanence itself, or the body without organs as it is also sometimes known.

The fact that all the mechanisms of defence – and I do believe the psychoanalytic diagnosis is warranted – mentioned above, from the stipulation of early and later, through the fantasy of an apostasy, to the denial of intellectual consistency, are motivated by a single enigma, namely de Certeau's religiosity, presents its own problems of course. Despite repeated affirmations of his Christianity, both direct and indirect, none more compelling I suppose than the simple fact that he never renounced his Jesuitical affiliation (even if he did eventually drop the telltale 'SJ' after his name), the enigma remains alive as ever because de Certeau constantly questioned the meaning of such an affirmation. He made belief his very topic of inquiry and perhaps by doing so made it seem that he himself no longer believed, as though to say that as soon as one exposes such a wan metaphysical concern to the bleaching light of scientific method one must surely be led to recant any attachment to it. In other words, atheism predisposes certain of de Certeau's readers to think he must have turned away from God because according to their own convictions that is the only way they can think well of him. Yet, as I will argue, no such turning away occurred. That said, a purely theological (or, at any rate, an exclusively 'religious studies') reading of de Certeau's work is equally unsatisfactory because it can only accommodate de Certeau's doubt in religious terms, as the proper – and quintessentially Catholic – questioning of the limits of one's faith, when in fact it seems to have run far deeper than that.[6]

De Certeau made belief an historical, philosophical, political as well as purely existential concern, and the full pluridimensionality (as I would want to call it) of his investigations needs to be considered if it is to be understood. Of course, saying it is one thing and doing it quite another. Inevitably, a reduction of some sort must be made, it being impossible (save in a Borgesian fantasy) to reproduce point for point in a single tome every nuance of a body of work spanning more than twenty volumes. By the same token, the very point of producing a study of an author is precisely to tender such a reduction of their body of work, so it would defeat the purpose of the exercise if one did in fact try simply to reproduce it point for point. Given that a reproduction is as undesirable as it is impossible, the key question is what type of reduction will be made, and what justification can be given? Such a question, as Deleuze has pointed out (1994: xix), is as much a matter of modesty as method, for it involves stipulating as fully and frankly as one can just what it is one wants to achieve. I should say then, that my aim, following a model inaugurated by Deleuze, is to produce de Certeau's double, his body without organs in other words. A double is made up of the set of presuppositions an author could not do without, even if they never actually articulate them (Deleuze, 1994: xxi). As such, it refers to what is always already begun in their work, not its beginning, which comes later.[7] 'The concept is the beginning of philosophy, but the plane is its instituting' (Deleuze and Guattari, 1994: 41). Practically, it amounts to a kind of plateau, or plane of immanence, unique to them, on which their ideas and concepts circulate.

> The plane of immanence is not a concept that is or can be thought but rather the image of thought, the image thought gives itself of what it means to think, to make use of thought, to find one's bearings in thought. (Deleuze and Guattari, 1994: 37)

Now, it is true, in the case of someone like de Certeau, a manifestly Christian scholar, his beginnings are always religious, but it is by no means certain that his already begun is similarly constructed. By the same token, religiosity only describes the character of de Certeau's plane, and thinly at that. We still need to specify its mode of operation. Philosophers spend most of their time building this plane, Deleuze says, but that does not mean it is always readily visible, at least not in the way, say, a political platform is supposed to be. Indeed, an author's plane is precisely not a platform in this sense, it is not a starting point, as I've said, but the always already begun. Inasmuch as it might manifest itself as a certain style, or taste, a peculiar way of operating, it bears a resemblance to the sociological notion of disposition, but it is not unconscious like disposition is. It belongs, rather, to the order of the unthought, what Blanchot (1993) (and Foucault [1987] and Deleuze [1988] after him) holds to be the inner prickling of the conscious that sets thought in motion, but always from the outside because it is not 'of thought'.[8] Constructing one's plane, one's body without organs, means finding a way of getting outside of the enchained interiority of the oneself (the 'I') in such as way as to make these electrifying impulses available for use – it amounts to speaking in the 'fourth person singular', which is neither you nor me, or even them and us, but a dissolution of the very idea of the self, a splendid 'they' that is impersonal and pre-individual (Deleuze, 1990: 152). In the French intellectual tradition, a special place is held for Sade, in this respect, because he is seen by many (Bataille, Klossowski, Foucault, Deleuze, as well as de Certeau) as the one who managed – if not for the first time, then certainly to an unrivalled extent – to actually achieve this profound depersonalisation through his uncloaking of desire, his laying bare of its very bedrock.[9]

The 'fourth person singular' is a utopian notion – Deleuze explicitly connects it to Melville's utopian 'community of celibates' (1997: 84–7). It bespeaks the fantasy of being radically other to the way one is, to the way one feels one is condemned to be by the sheer fact of being human. But, more than that, and this is why I have said it is utopian, it also bespeaks a fantasy of a collective existence organised along very different lines to the one we are forced to live in today – it is not merely prior to late capitalism, as, say, antiquity is, but wholly other to it, and perhaps imaginable only in science fictional terms. Its first problem, therefore, is always one of credibility: the 'they' of this community that is always 'still to come' lacks a discourse that could make it believable, so it hides out in fantasy, in fiction, in dreams, where it is constrained to produce images of itself (LeGuin's Gethenians stand in the place of a truly genderless society). Creating a language for this people 'still to come', is, according to Kafka, the primary task of the minor author – that is, the revolutionary and utopian author who writes not for the sake of mass sales but to diagnose and indict a sick society.[10] The philosopher, meanwhile, must, for the same reason, construct the grounds of this revolutionary language's credibility by lifting it out of the dubious realms of the purely figural and finding it a form, a plane of its own devising. A plane of immanence is therefore the fantasy of a collective existence peculiar to a philosopher, their innermost 'they' in other words, which their writing cannot but betray, because like a return of the repressed, it is what secretly organises it.

Generally speaking, it manifests itself as consistency, as the glue which invisibly holds an agglomeration of concepts and ideas together, that is, as a quality not a quantity. This is why Deleuze is so attentive to the style of any philosophy, and I suspect it also explains de Certeau's similarly keen interest in the topic. Giard, for instance, suggests that the real reason, by which she means the genuinely impassioned reason, de Certeau finally rejected both Bourdieu's and Foucault's sociocultural models (habitus and discipline) in spite of their obvious resonances with his own enterprise is that he could not stomach their style.[11]

> A difference comes into play here that precedes theory, a distance that one might qualify as an *elective anti-affinity* and that does not impede interest or fascination in proposing theses. With these words, I am pointing something out that would characterise the entire inspiration of a kind of thinking, its 'style", its own tonality, in short its presuppositions, which do not stem from the critical awareness of the author and are never made explicit, but in which is rooted that which specifies a way of being in the world and rendering it intelligible. (Giard, 1998a: xxi)

What we see here, which will be extremely useful in trying to determine the nature of de Certeau's own style, is that taste is the complement, or to put it differently, the indirect expression, of style.[12] My implication is that an author's plane of immanence can be specified by drawing the diagram of their tastes and distastes, never explained preferences and undefended choices – religious belief is precisely one such undefended choice. And, what is more, this diagram will invariably depict a fantasised form of collective existence.

Drawing the diagram of an author's plane of immanence means grasping their work as a whole, which, in Deleuze's view (1995: 85), is the equivalent of denying oneself the luxury of picking and choosing. One grasps an oeuvre as a whole as soon as one knows what its primary problematic is, what it is, in other words, that animates it (the always already begun). The working assumption is that beneath the exquisite variety of topics and concerns an oeuvre as rich as de Certeau's displays there is a bedrock that is, by comparison, strikingly singular in vision and purpose. This is the plane of immanence. We get to it by asking, at every turn, why should an author want to say that?[13] It is not, however, a simple matter of supposing in the classical hermeneutic fashion that there is always a deeper, hidden layer of meaning beneath whatever we take to be the surface of the text, which by virtue of its depth is the true meaning, because this particular bedrock is dynamic. Far from being a truth, in the last instance, as it were, the plane of immanence is calculating, selective and differentiating, in the first instance, and finds itself dramatised in the question 'why?'. God, in this respect, can never correspond to the plane of immanence exactly, since that would imply the philosopher was the cause of God, which is impossible. God's role can only be that of supporting authority. So, in the place of traditional inquiries into the influences an author's work displays, we are instead asking what form of life (collective existence) does the work correspond to, and why would the author want to take that stand? And although I have used Deleuze here to explicate this line of inquiry, it is not, I believe, alien to de Certeau at all because what are 'ways of operating' (de Certeau's great catchcry) if not forms of life?

Having staked out a method of inquiry, which to give it a name, finally, may be called noology, we can now move to the pressing question of the constitution of de Certeau's plane of immanence.[14] At this point, I do not want to attempt anything more than a sketch outline, it being the task of the remaining chapters to provide a fuller picture. That said, it has to be admitted that the difficulty faced here is formidable, for in effect what is being searched for is precisely that which by definition is absent but nevertheless present on an organisational level. Again, though, we hear echoes of de Certeau here too because one of his chief interests was the absent in history and the way they return in other forms, under new guises (for example, see de Certeau et al., 1998: 251). For now, then, I want to turn to a very short paper de Certeau originally wrote for a special issue of *Architecture intérieure/Créé* on 'Paris, le retour de la ville', called 'Ghosts in the City', which, in my view, brings into focus something that I will argue is to be found throughout his work and can therefore be said to indicate (though not to constitute) his plane of immanence (see de Certeau et al., 1998: 133–43). From the tone of this piece, which is openly urging, one gets the feeling that de Certeau took seriously the opportunity of writing for (and to, I guess it should also be said) professional architects and that he felt more was at stake than the elegance of the writing or the sophistication of the ideas expressed. This piece has a nakedness about it that makes it quite instructive, I think, without it being either exceptional or anomalous. De Certeau wrote a number of papers for governmental agencies, such as the OECD (for whom he produced a report on immigration and schooling) that have a similar rawness (see for example, 1997a: 143–74).

Ostensibly, 'Ghosts in the City' is a paper about the architecture of renovation, specifically the re-use of old buildings, and the renewal of certain urban dead spots such as old dock areas, but from the title one can already sense an ambivalence toward its topic that as one reads on quickly cements itself as the governing motif – the new is not welcome unless it supports, protects and, better, fosters the present by respecting the past. If it does not heed these imperatives, de Certeau's conviction is that the ghosts of yesteryear (past fashions fully as much as past lives) will not be able to haunt the new space and it will therefore prove unlivable. Nothing could be less inviting to de Certeau than a space built on a genuinely clear slate. His taste is decidedly in favour of the palimpsest – we need ghosts, de Certeau thinks. 'More than its utilitarian and technocratic transparency, it is the opaque ambivalence of its oddities that makes the city livable. A new baroque seems to be taking the place of the rational geometries that repeated the same forms everywhere and that geographically clarified the distinction of functions (commerce, leisure, schools, housing, etc.)' (de Certeau et al., 1998: 134). But the vain and grandiose perpetrators of fresh start architecture, such as Le Corbusier, surely one of de Certeau's targets here, are not the only culprits in the ongoing crime that to his mind is urban planning. Similarly distasteful to him is the apparently opposite pole of an assiduous preservation of past glories.

The trouble with this practice is its fetishistic character: it is selective, hypostatising, even idolising, and through being so it museumifies the city in such a way as to make it a showcase of the dead instead of a stage for the living:

> It is not that the museum is a plague or that it can be transformed into a scarecrow or a scapegoat. The museum often exercises the role of laboratory, ahead of urban planning. But it functions in its own way. It conceals from users what it presents to observers. It stems from a theatrical, pedagogical, and/or scientific operation that pulls objects away from their everyday use (from yesterday or today), objects that it offers up to curiosity, information, or analysis. (de Certeau et al., 1998: 138)

In other words, in its very apprehension and presentation of cultural objects the museum apparatus enforces a change of register akin to the one the fetishist accomplishes by sexualising select appurtenances of the body (boots, underclothes, fur capes and so forth). By concentrating all their attention on the body's associative material, but not the body itself, the fetishist elevates it to such an extent that this paraphernalia can stand in the place of the body and function in the same way within the limited confines of sexual arousal. Similarly, the museum lifts everyday items out of the everyday realm, making them seem exceptional and important instead of ordinary and useful; it also confines the range of uses cultural objects may have by making them 'interesting', 'curious' and 'informative'.

But however disastrous these two practices may be, so long as they are grounded in aesthetics they are not nearly so devastating as the alternative, namely an architecture driven by a virile, entrepreneurial capitalism:

> If one refuses to accept the logic of conservation, what other hypothesis will take over? When the museum pulls back, what wins? The *law of the market*. Such is the alternative presented to the interventions of the state and the Paris city hall: they must either uphold the institutions of preservation (more or less pedagogical), both public (museums) and private (associations and hobbies of all sorts), or enter into the production-consumption system (real-estate agencies, project developers, architectural firms). (de Certeau et al., 1998: 138)

In recent times, downtowns, more or less everywhere, but particularly in the older, what some call post-industrial cities, have been swooped upon by developers, their crumbling factories and warehouses rubbed back and restored and converted into up-market apartments and shopping malls (Jameson, 1994: 25; 1998: 185). And this is precisely what de Certeau did not want to see happen because it displaces existing communities, forcing them to disperse into the outer suburbs where brand new instruments of urban isolation await them (think of the notorious low-cost housing 'projects' of the 1960s).[15] Gentrification, as this roseate form of urban blight is also known as, is, on de Certeau's view, colonisation by another name – it alters buildings and lives alike, but not equally beneficially.

> Through its own movement, the restoration economy tends to separate places from their practitioners. A misappropriation of subjects accompanies the renovation of objects. More than from malicious intentions, this movement results from the very logic of an apparatus (technical and scientific) that is constituted by isolating the treatment of objects from the subject's consideration. In this particular case, it is not surprising that technical administrations are so interested in buildings and so little in the inhabitants, or that, for example in a time of recession that requires a struggle against the degradation of existing buildings, they grant things capable of resisting time a value that they refuse to elderly people. They select and manage what they are equipped for – which concerns a production or a restoration of objects. (de Certeau et al., 1998: 139)

It is the 'clinical' (as de Certeau comes to see it) separation of lives and buildings that restoration implies which de Certeau objects to most

strongly because of the way it fails to respect that a place of residence is
not merely where one happens to live, but the place where one's life is
made.[16] According to de Certeau, the underpinning impetus in the
restoration economy is part and parcel of a generalised medicalisation
of power: 'This power is becoming more and more a "nursing" power.
It takes responsibility for the health of the social body and thus for its
mental, biological, or urban illnesses. It gives itself the task, and the
right, to cure, protect, and educate' (de Certeau et al., 1998: 139). His
view of medicine is very similar to Foucault's (perhaps it is not
surprising, then, that he says *Madness and Civilisation* and *The Birth of
the Clinic* are Foucault's best books [1986: 172]). Like Foucault, he
finds the medical gaze to be as ruthlessly dissecting and ultimately as
inhumane (by which I mean, more concerned with knowing death, than
learning about life) as the scalpel it wields.[17] And the sharpest cut of all
is the one presumed to be made between the patient and the person – the
therapist, on this view, is only able to treat the former to the extent that
they ignore the latter, and even then they must guard against thinking
of the patient as a whole, as something greater than the sum of their
wounds and ailments, for to do so would be to lose all objectivity and
cloud judgement.

With this last, rather bizarre analogy, matching medicine and real-
estate speculation, we come to what I believe is the crux of the matter.
In particular, there are two points I want to highlight: first, de Certeau
is clearly suspicious of anything that smacks at all of utopian thinking
(medicine, fully as much as urban renewal); and, second, he is quite
desperate in his plea-making that a certain ineffable something of
everyday life be consciously conserved by architects and city-planners
alike (the person that lingers on in spite of being treated as a patient).
Both of these themes are to be found everywhere in de Certeau's work.
The city, de Certeau argues, is a richly-textured fabric woven by its
users: it comprises of buildings and streets, obviously, but also people
and their gestures (ways of operating), their ways of walking, the places
they stop to chat with old friends, the pleasure they take in a well-
tended lawn, or a carefully clipped hedge, as well as the stories they tell
one another and the dreams they nurture in their hearts.[18] It is this
precious fabric that restoration – or, for that matter, any determined
intervention into city-life – threatens to destroy, if it does not heed the
fact that a city is as much mythic as it is material, which means
recognising that its skeleton of bricks and mortar is suffused with a
spirit comprised of the ghosts of countless lives (de Certeau et al., 1998:
143).

At first glance, it might appear that these two poles contradict one
another, because anti-utopia seems antipathetic to the apparent
utopianism of an ineffable something that is resistant to the last degree.
Yet, in fact, they spring from one and the same impulse because utopia

– the Marxist version – means radical change, the kind of change that sweeps away all resistances; it is therefore utopia itself that this ineffable something resists (no matter that its face may be fascist and totalitarian: as is often said nowadays even the Nazis were utopian to begin with). Even in a situation as utopian-charged as May 1968 must have been, at least at a libidinal level, a time when in de Certeau's own perception, it seemed as if a radical change had in fact occurred, that somehow the old had been exposed in a new light that destroyed its credibility, opening the space for a new way of thinking about society to briefly blossom, de Certeau still did not take an avowedly utopian position.[19] What he saw instead was that the ineffable something he'd long had faith in was suddenly being released into the wind – people were 'starting to speak' – and that was what was truly marvellous about the 'events' (de Certeau, 1997a: 11). Communication had become possible, again (his model being that of the relation, thought lost, between man and the word of God), and this, de Certeau felt, despite the patently obvious (depressing to some) fact that society would not be changed at a superstructural level in any meaningful or lasting way by the 'events', was something to be 'understood'.[20]

If he shied away from utopian discourse in this heady period it was because he saw that it tended to cloud issues, but more importantly, it choked back this voice he was hearing for the first time. So long as people spoke 'in the name of' – a doctrine, a dogma, a party, a politics, utopia, whatever – they were not speaking 'for themselves'; yet this is precisely what was most radical about the 'events', the fact that people were 'starting to speak' (de Certeau, 1997a: 15). Somewhat startlingly, then, what we discover here is that for de Certeau, communication – the ideal speech situation, man in contact with God – is held to contradict utopia. His suspicion of utopia, we now see, stems from the fact that he perceives in the fabled 'ineffable something' a literally greater power (resistance is something like the mystical sign, it indicates the presence of God). This 'ineffable something' is, of course, simply the repressed form of communication, the ideal speech situation driven inwards by the destruction of its contextual parameters (belief in God, for instance). His rhetoric of spectres, witnessed above, we may now conclude is designed to remind us of the irrepressibility – in the last degree – of this particular form of ideality; by utilising a centuries old scenario taken from the historical popular imagination, which under the rubric of the gothic, and in the form of the ghost story, gave us a notion of the return of the repressed long before Freud came along and named it, de Certeau is able to postulate a form of resistance resistant to reason.

> The ghost story is indeed virtually the architecture genre par excellence, wedded as it is to rooms and buildings ineradicably stained with the memory of gruesome events, material structures in which the past

literally 'weighs like a nightmare on the brain of the living'. (Jameson, 1998: 187)

Todorov conceptualises this genre for us, conveniently enough, under the 'auratic' sign of the 'fantastic' – which can be anything, he says, that causes us to hesitate in deciding between a natural and a supernatural explanation of an occurrence (1973: 25). My description of it as 'auratic', is less to do with its content, however, than its function. The 'fantastic' (in all its forms, including the ghostly, the uncanny, even the mystical) is, I want to suggest, equivalent in its use to the function that, on Jameson's reading of them, 'aura' has in Benjamin and 'mimesis' has in Adorno. Literally defined as 'the unique phenomenon of a distance' (Benjamin, 1968: 222), 'aura' is the opposite of immediacy; or, as it is perhaps better to say, 'aura' is what governs immediacy (in the sense that steam engines have governors) because it is what protects it from self annihilation (Eagleton, 1981: 39). Without this distance we could not distinguish original from copy, the authentic from the fake, and of course it is precisely this power of discrimination that has been lost to us in modern times, thanks to mechanical reproduction. Moreover, it is this distance, which in the late capitalist thrall of commodity aesthetics we seem at equal pains to destroy as to preserve, that distinguishes our language from the word of God. His word knows no such distance, and has no need of it either because it is properly immediate.

In de Certeau's case, the concept of 'haunting' is itself magical because through rehearsing one of His effects it can stand in the place of God in a time apparently bereft of His presence.[21] In this sense, it is quite correct to classify it as an 'auratic' term because it aspires to 'authorise' a discourse with its self-proclaimed authenticity, originality and rarity. Here I want to highlight the fact that it is the very terms 'ghostly', 'uncanny', and so forth that are the truly fantastical elements in de Certeau's discourse, and not their putative referents. It is these fantastic terms themselves that introduce that critical form of hesitancy we call ambiguity into de Certeau's texts, what in his own language should be described as heterological because it plays, for its own gain, on the present absence of an other. In critical terms, as Jameson makes clear, what such terms do, in fact, is introduce a pleasant seeming fog that obscures the origins of terms in such a way as to make them feel natural, grounded and true. 'It is as though', he says, in writers like Benjamin and Adorno (to which short-list I would add de Certeau's name), 'a kind of repressed foundational longing found its way back into their writing by way of these magical terms, which are evoked to explain everything without ever themselves being explained, until at length we become persuaded that they could never themselves be explained or grounded, and mark the root of some archaic private obsession, as in Ur-sounds and names of the great modern poets' (Jameson, 1990: 64).[22]

Haunting is an image that recurs frequently in de Certeau's writing, often at the start of books (*The Writing of History* and *The Possession of Loudun*).[23] It is used to create a stereoscopy demanding the text be read in, as it were, two minds – one attuned to the crisp rationality of the lucid exposé of a peculiar historical period (the seventeenth-century) or occurrence (the possession and exorcism of an entire convent), and another attendant to the bewildering coruscations of a twittering 'other' life. While it is tempting to read this stereoscopy dialectically, there are no authentic grounds to do so.[24] In de Certeau's presentation of it, what one mind is asked to contemplate, namely history, is nowhere contradicted by what the other mind has to consider, namely the 'other' – the two stand side by side, equally possible, equally plausible. Since they are not of the same realm, the one cannot cancel the other, though it can suppress it, nor cannot it be relieved of it either, except temporarily (one may forget it, disguise it, ignore it, but it will always return). The relation is nearer to a syllogism than a contradiction, though it isn't quite that either since that would amount to an automatic supposition of otherness when in fact it is the haunting suspicion of its existence that is at issue. But, inasmuch as it is a truly gothic scene that de Certeau is trying to present, it is a return not of individual anxieties, personal angsts, or singular fears (all of which are latter day, Freudian interpolations anyway), that he has in mind, but the generalised trembling 'they' feel in the face of the supernatural. In their uncanniness, ghosts represent the scandal of the emptying of speech of God's word, they render visible yet unearthly what had formerly given discourse its thickness.

The question we must now ask, is why de Certeau should be so adamant utopia is not merely different from the ideal speech situation, but somehow deleterious, that he should feel the need to pit ghosts against it? In short, how is it that utopia is seen to contradict communication, when on first appearances anyway utopia would seem to be the best name for the ideal speech situation of which de Certeau speaks so insistently? It is surely utopian to imagine a society changed such that no one's speech is suppressed by anyone else's. Yet de Certeau does not see it that way at all; in fact, on the contrary, he consistently paints utopia as a threat against which his ghosts of ordinary-lives past must fight a rearguard action. Whence the fear? Since de Certeau does not address this question specifically, we are forced to extrapolate an answer for ourselves. I follow Jameson in thinking there is, to use his words, 'no more pressing task for progressive people in the First World than tirelessly to analyse and diagnose the fear and anxiety before Utopia itself' (1994: 61). I also think, as I have argued throughout, that such anxiety must have as its root cause a deep-seated indisposition, which is to say, anxiety must always be treated as symptomatic of an 'other' scene (or to put it another way, a 'form of life' still to come) which it is the task of the analyst to produce. Following Deleuze, I have referred to this 'other' scene as the plane of immanence. What I want to suggest now is that insofar as our speculative answer to the above question (why is de Certeau so fearful of utopia?) can be shown to issue from a coherently constructed 'faculty' (for the want of a better word) then we may rightly say we have adduced de Certeau's plane of immanence.

This presents a methodological problem, for while we know well the shape and colour of the peculiar symptoms whose cause we now seek (de Certeau is a Christian scholar, he is evidently anti-utopian, and he holds to a notion of ineradicable resistance), we do not know how to make the leap from them to the 'disease' itself. The risk is, of course, that any such leap as we may make will turn out to have been nothing but a projection, our own wish-fulfilment masquerading as a reasoned answer. Freud's greatness rests on the fact that he was able to systematise his intuitions with sufficient formality to call them a theory, but as countless admirers and detractors have said since: one has to be Freud to make the at times astonishing leaps of imagination he makes. Indeed, Lacan suggests that it is Freud's heedlessness of his own doctrine that is both the basis of his success as an individual analyst and the single most taunting provocation in his work, which even today, at least in the eyes of the more programmatic-minded scholars, makes his work seem scandalous (1977: 77). Similarly, de Certeau has illustrated that there is always an unreproducible element of 'tact' to Freud's analyses that is unique to him (1988: 304). Primarily, as both Lacan and de Certeau emphasise, Freud's subjective presence in his doctrine and its resulting aleatory quality is due to the fact that psychoanalysis is born of the therapeutic situation; the ongoing transformations in the relations between Freud and his patients have been recorded for posterity in his case histories where they are registered more as a constant form of variance than an unchanging algorithm (Lacan, 1977: 78; de Certeau, 1986: 20). It is in view of precisely this type of superficial inconsistency that a notion like the plane of immanence becomes invaluable because it is unaffected by the relatively minor shifts involved in the diastole and systole of the everyday life of a theory.

Not surprisingly, then, what Deleuze calls Freud to account for has nothing at all to do with the tactical quality of his analyses (though at times, he is moved to lament Freud's tactlessness with his patients – he obviously never listened to them, Deleuze cries!).[25] Deleuze's criticism is aimed directly at Freud's plane of immanence when he calls him to account for the fact that – in Deleuze's view – he erroneously treats the stifled desires and displaced fears represented by the so-called Oedipal-complex (i.e., desire for the mother and fear of castration by the father) as a cause when it is in fact a symptom. Freud's error, Deleuze argues, is to go along with the 'common-sense' assumption that if a thing (incest) is prohibited it must first of all be desired; that, in effect, the fact of the prohibition is proof of the desire (Deleuze and Guattari, 1983: 70). A prohibition, even one so rigorously policed as the incest taboo, says 'nothing about an original reality of desire because it essentially disfigures the desired' (Deleuze and Guattari, 1983: 161). In other words, by going along with the 'common-sense' view, Freud failed to heed one of his own lessons: desire rarely exhibits itself in its utmost nudity, especially when it is repressed. Deleuze's claim, which is a keystone in his 'schizoanalytic' cultural hermeneutics, is that incest refers to an already disfigured desire, a desire, what's more, that the law against it has shaped to suit its own 'mythic' needs. Incest, in practice, is a social structure's way of coding desire ('disfiguring') in order to make it susceptible to repression.

The incest prohibition represents society's fear of unrestrained desire, according to Deleuze, and its purpose is to code the free exercise of desire as 'dark', atavistic and unreasonable, so as to teach us to fear it and subsequently to willingly accept its repression. What the taboo does is transform desire in general (call it the libido, polymorphic perversity, or what you will) into a specific desire (call it sexual, or even genital) which it can then claim is in need of direction. Incest is thus a repressing representation – it is a cautionary image extolling the dangers of free desire standing in the place of genuinely free desire. Freud's analyses, on this view, can thus be said to have stopped a couple of steps too soon. Deleuze may be likened then to a hero in one of those fantastic boy's own tales which always suppose there is another cave beyond the one the grave-robbers have already ransacked which contains the *real* crown jewels. As all action heroes do, he knows when he is being decoyed, and he knows to dig a little deeper. But as a scholar, he also knows that the key to any puzzle is not found by striking at the greatest depth, but by a careful scrutiny of what is right there on the surface, if only one can see how the surface is constituted:

> Let us remember once again one of Marx's caveats: we cannot tell from the mere taste of wheat who grew it; the product gives us no hint as to the system and the relations of production. The product appears to be all the more specific, incredibly specific and readily describable, the more closely the theoretician relates it to *ideal forms of causation, comprehension, or expression*, rather than to *the real process of production on which it depends*. (Deleuze and Guattari, 1983: 24)

With this problem in mind, then, I want to utilise as an hermeneutic device, Deleuze's five-point explanation of the way incest is used to repress desire (Deleuze and Guattari, 1983: 266).

The baseline here is of course desire in a free state: it is given somewhat magical properties by Deleuze – just one drop, he says, is enough to put all of society into a chaotic death spin (Deleuze and Guattari, 1983: 116). His image of this unrestricted form of desire is schizophrenia, the process rather than the illness. Less prosaically, though, desire is simply another name for the *absolute limit* of a system, in this case the social system. It is that flux in which the social is suspended and must differentiate itself by power of its organisation; as such, it isn't terribly surprising that a society should want to do all that it can to keep it at bay. The social system itself, which Deleuze always equates with what Marxism refers to as the mode of production (in our time this means late capitalism), is the corresponding *relative limit*: it is what ceases to exist if the *absolute limit* is transgressed. By this reckoning, desire is also the *exterior limit* of capitalism, the ghostly presence of the 'outside' (all that could crush capitalism were it left unchecked – equitable labour laws and so forth) which suffuses the living body ('inside') of capitalism and must therefore be constantly repelled and exorcised. Its way of warding of this *exterior limit* is to institute a battery of its own *immanent limits*, boundary points that if respected will for ever stave off absolute freedom (the concept of debt is undoubtedly the most effective of these). In order to manage the threat posed by the *absolute limit* the social system has to find a means of internalising it, domesticating it into a serviceable *interior limit*: 'Oedipus is this displaced or internalised limit where desire lets itself be caught' (Deleuze and Guattari, 1983: 266).

Let's see now if this can assist us in giving a more definite shape to de Certeau's plane of immanence. If we remember that the *absolute limit* is actually Deleuze's ideal, that is desire in its free state, then we will have no difficulty in asserting that de Certeau's *absolute limit* must be 'communication' (in the idealised sense he gives it) because it is, similarly, the ideal against which he measures everything else. By the same token, therefore, his *relative limit* must similarly be the state and its organs, for as we see in his comments on city-planning it is precisely the state that he holds responsible for preserving the city's vitality. The *exterior limit* of the state would be communication's many residues, all the practices and ways of operating that we have until now collected under the general rubric of that ineffable something. The state is haunted by what it cannot articulate: hence it plans, calculates and conceptualises, constantly, in an effort to measure its perimeters and, as it were, take its own temperature (de Certeau, 1984: 94). These are its *immanent limits*. Finally, and perhaps the most controversially, I want to suggest that de Certeau's *interior limit*, that which domesticates the *absolute limit* is utopia itself. Utopia, in de Certeau's construction of it, is precisely a disfigured and dishonoured form of communication; it is always seen to be an instrument of the state apparatus, usually as an ideological means of suppressing individual creativity (de Certeau frequently correlates administration with utopia [1984: 94]). So, to paraphrase Deleuze, utopia is the displaced or internalised limit where communication lets itself be caught: it is not merely different from communication, utopia is the lure that prevents us from attaining it.

My implication is that communication is the platform on which all of de Certeau's thinking rests: the absolute limit and the plane of immanence are one and the same (Deleuze and Guattari, 1994: 38). Although it serves the same function that, in a different era, would have been God's role, namely the securing of discourse, it stands in a different place and is organised immanently not transcendentally. It is this transformation of the way religious discourse is constructed that needs to be grappled with if de Certeau's religiosity is to be properly understood. As Deleuze notes, religious philosophers have difficulty constructing their planes of immanence because they need to posit at least one transcendental term, God, which undoes the whole fabric.[26] For the same reason, it should also be said, religious philosophers can never be truly utopian – they cannot countenance either perfection on earth or the absolute nihilism of starting over, both of which are God's provenance. By the same token, societies confronting their absolute limit see in it a sign of the imminent death. For, in the case of ideal communication, at least, its arrival would spell the instant end of all the protective institutions we have built around our various imperfect forms of communication, from the judiciary to legislature: 'Such is the *real limit*' (Deleuze and Guattari, 1983: 176). Anti-utopia is thus not so much anti-change as against change made in the name of a false god, utopia.

In the place of a hope for radical change engineered by human hands, de Certeau is thus compelled to offer – while he awaits God's intervention – a series of pragmatic suggestions for change in our time, hence, no doubt, his willingness to cooperate in ventures like the European Colloquium on cultural development (Arc-et-Senans, April 1972).[27] That being said, it is worth noting, as Eagleton (1981) reminds us, that cultural critics in this century produce their work in time when class struggle has already been effectively quashed. So while it may be fair to say de Certeau's pragmatism is somewhat defeatist in outlook, it is equally fair to say that his pragmatism is what revolutionary criticism looks like today. Far from having his head stuck in the clouds, de Certeau tends to operate at the level of the immanent limits: the all too earthly realm of government policy. He uses the interior limit, utopia, to draw our attention to the tragic frailty of policy, to the fact that a grandiose vision alone is not sufficient to ameliorate the living conditions of anyone, and that, as with the case of low-cost housing in the 1960s, such utopian ideas as either the 'radiant city' (Le Corbusier) or the 'garden city' (Howard) can prove disastrous if they take no account of actual living conditions, but stick instead with their own lofty ideals of 'space'.[28] Of course, in the case of someone like Le Corbusier, it wasn't so much that he didn't understand living conditions as loathed them and felt the only means of rectification was renewal preceded by destruction (Berman, 1988: 165–9). While unimpressed by utopias – false Gods, by another name, in his book – de Certeau is exceptionally optimistic in his views of what can be achieved by practical means through soundly researched and flexibly administered policy.

Notes

[1] Jameson's provocative suggestion (1999: 268) that it was Walter Benjamin's good fortune not to be immediately and fully translated into English does not hold for de Certeau.

[2] The first translation to be noticed by cultural studies was a section of what would subsequently be published as *The Practice of Everyday Life* (de Certeau, 1980a). Interestingly enough, the translation was inaugurated by Fredric Jameson. Even more interesting, though, is the fact that since then Jameson has not made significant mention of de Certeau's work anywhere within his own oeuvre; this is startling, in a way, because Jameson has written about virtually every other French scholar of note, making us wonder why he should choose to make an exception of de Certeau.

[3] For an extended critique of Ahearne, see Buchanan, 1996a.

[4] 'Certeau has left us, in the words of Jean Louis Schefer, with "the image of an open work"' (Ahearne, 1995: 3).

[5] For instance, both Mike Davis and Fredric Jameson consider themselves Marxists, but that does not mean they are able to find much to agree upon between them: Davis (1985) attacks totalisation in the name of Marxism, and Jameson (1991) defends it on the same grounds.

[6] For a range of religious readings of de Certeau see Ward, 1996; Geffré, 1991; and Le Brun, 1988.

[7] For the distinction between 'beginnings' and 'the already begun', see Deleuze and Guattari, 1983: 91.

[8] 'The outside is not a fixed limit but a moving matter animated by the peristaltic movements, folds and foldings that together make up an inside: they are not something other than the outside, but precisely the inside *of* the outside. *The Order of Things* developed this theme: if thought comes from outside, and remains attached to the outside, how come the outside does not flood into the inside, as the element that thought does not and cannot think of? The unthought is therefore not external to thought but lies at its very heart, as that impossibility of thinking which doubles or hollows out the outside' (Deleuze, 1988: 96–7).

[9] 'In the age of Kant and Hegel, at a time when the interiorisation of the law of history and the world was being imperiously demanded by Western consciousness as never before, Sade gives voice to the nakedness of desire as the lawless law of the world' (Foucault, 1987: 17).

[10] For a definition of minor writing and minor authors, see Deleuze and Guattari, 1986: 16–27.

[11] For a different, 'spatial', meditation on the elective disaffinities between de Certeau and Bourdieu, see Thrift 1996: 14–16.

[12] For an important and complementary analysis of de Certeau's style, see Carrard, 1992.

[13] 'Any given concept, feeling or belief will be treated as symptoms of a will that wills something. What does *the one that* says this, that thinks or feels that, will? It is a matter of showing that he could not say, think or feel this particular thing if he did not a particular will, particular forces, a particular way of being. What he will the one who speaks, loves or creates?' (Deleuze, 1983: 78).

[14] Noology, as Jameson explains (1997: 405), is the new name for what in the vernacular of Marxism is called *Ideologiekritik*.

[15] 'The renovated blocks form ghettos for well-off people, and the real-estate curettages are thus becoming "segregative operations"' (de Certeau, 1998: 139).

[16] On this point, it is worth noting that Deleuze's (1989) notion of a clinical method stands in direct opposition to all forms of medicalisation; it holds the medical notion of the clinical to be something of a perversion of a noble art.

[17] As Foucault puts it, the 'constitution of pathological anatomy at the period when the clinicians were defining their method is no mere coincidence: the balance of experience required that the gaze directed upon the individual and the language of description should rest upon the stable, visible, legible basis of death' (1973: 196).

[18] 'Gestures are the true archives of the city, if one understands by "archives" the past that is selected and reused according to present custom. They remake the urban landscape every day' (de Certeau et al., 1998: 141).

[19] His conclusion, which appears utopian to me, was, as follows: 'I see a new and important sociocultural phenomenon in the impact of the expression that demonstrates a disarticulation between what is *said* and what is *unsaid*, that deprives a social practice of its tacit foundations, that ultimately refers, I believe, to a displacement of "values" on which an architecture of powers and exchanges had been constructed and that was still assumed to be a solid base' (de Certeau, 1997a: 8).

[20] De Certeau makes exactly the same demand of the 'events' at Loudun in the years 1632–1640. Before we make judgements, he says, we must first try to understand what actually happened (1996a: 7–16).

[21] As such it is accurate, though not terribly helpful in my opinion, to think heterology under the sign of negative ontology, as Ricoeur (1988: 150) does in his rather cursory examination of de Certeau.

[22] '"Aura" and "mimesis" are therefore the hostages given to the unique and the particular which free an extraordinary universalising thought and language to go about its business' (Jameson, 1990: 64).

[23] For a preliminary survey of the use of 'haunting' metaphors in de Certeau's work, see Buchanan, 1996a: 149.

[24] For a description of the proper conditions for a dialectic stereoscopy, see Jameson, 1990: 28.

[25] 'The trap was set from the start: never will the Wolf-Man speak. Talk as he might about wolves, howl as he might like a wolf, Freud does not

even listen; he glances at his dog and answers. "It's daddy"' (Deleuze and Guattari, 1987: 38).

[26] 'Religious authority wants immanence to be tolerated only locally or at an intermediary level, a little like a terraced fountain where water can briefly immanate on each level but on condition that it comes from a higher source and falls lower down (transcendence and transdescendence, as Wahl said)' (Deleuze and Guattari, 1994: 45).

[27] De Certeau was the principal moderator for this colloquium. The text of his inaugural lecture is reproduced in *Culture in the Plural*.

[28] Undoubtedly the best critic of such muddled-headed utopias as either the 'radiant city' or 'garden city' is Jane Jacobs (1961). De Certeau's suspicion of utopia would seem to parallel that of Jacobs inasmuch as they both equate it with the 'impractical', or worse, the 'unlived'.

2. 'Blasting Free', or, The Stylistic Inflection[1]

In philosophy as in literature the distinction between something expressed and the means or form through which it is expressed is archaic: there is no incorrect formulation of a true idea; the search for the proper expression is the same as the search for the wholly adequate notion.

Fredric Jameson, *Sartre: The Origins of a Style*

We were able to derive a picture of de Certeau's plane of immanence by focusing our attention on certain undefended choices he made in the elaboration of his concepts. In effect, we concentrated on what – according to the vernacular of the Freudian method we ostensibly deployed (it being the deeper argument of the chapter that Deleuze and Guattari's method is still Freudian, however anti-oedipal it purports to be) – may usefully be called 'slips', that is, unconscious prejudices which have somehow slipped past the gatekeeper in the preconscious and found their way into print. What I want to turn to now, then, under the broad rubric of 'style', is the conscious choices de Certeau made in his work. I want to try to 'understand' de Certeau's plane of immanence by analysing its stylistic inflections. My rationale is that an analysis style is at the same time an elucidation of a method because, in our time, according to Jameson at least, 'the search for the proper expression is the same as the search for the wholly adequate notion' (1961: 67). On the evidence of a number of imaginative language experiments de Certeau conducted in his own writing, not to mention the exceptionally rigorous analyses of other authors' styles he was to write himself, I will take it as read that de Certeau was conscious of the importance and effect of style and argue that in an objective or purely formal sense his own rhetoric can *and should* be taken as reflecting this consciousness. At which point, what becomes interesting in his work is not merely the 'concepts' and their respective places in the critical arsenal, but how they manage 'to get said in the first place, and at what price' (Jameson, 1990: 10).

'Understanding' is a term de Certeau himself used to describe precisely the kind of non-judgemental criticism Foucault dreamt of.[2] In rehearsing it here I am attempting to stage my argument in a form consonant with its object, such that the encounter and its fruit will be one and the same. As a mode of inquiry, 'understanding' comes to our attention in the same moment as 'communication' does, which, conveniently enough, can therefore serve to define the historical conditions that produced it. I am of course referring to de Certeau's accounts of the 'Events' of May 1968, which are framed by this singular ambition to understand: 'We have to come back to this "thing" that happened and *understand* what the unpredictable taught us about ourselves, that is, what, since then, we have become' (de Certeau, 1997a: 4; my emphasis). But that isn't going to be easy, he muses, because in effect what happened was the unthinkable – it was a rupture, a sudden shift of allegiances, a seismic cultural event, not the inevitable product of unrest, nor the culmination of long years of fomentation, such as most revolutions can usually be seen to have been.[3] Understanding the unthinkable calls for a new approach to cultural analysis, de Certeau argues, because the old methods are bound to try to map it to pre-existing criteria which by definition are inapplicable to the genuinely new, which in his view the 'Events' of May 1968 proved themselves to be.[4] But since it lacks a name, I am going to call this proposed approach (for the want of a better word): 'understanding'.

> To the very extent that it happened upon us the way it did, the event has to teach us how to cast doubt on mental habits or social reflexes that would lead us to call it meaningless or to forget its significance. From an epistemological point of view, the event puts on the agenda of every discipline a new task, a task that cannot be dissociated from a pedagogical relation, that is, a relation with the other. The reintroduction of this *relation* into science is the same problem as that of the *event* in a reflection that is too imprisoned by the development of a system. (de Certeau, 1997a: 4)

What we see here is that the central task of 'understanding' is finding the critical means of making interpretations a function of the events themselves. That being the case, our first question will likely be what distinguishes 'understanding' from mere impressionism? For surely that is what it means to let the event dictate its own interpretation, because all one is able to fall back on in such a situation is one's own senses. Selection of data appears then to be merely accidental or otherwise happenstance, not carefully chosen, self-validating and vindicated – as it seems strangely apposite to add. But, as Jameson argues in a very early work, defending an equally impressionistic-seeming approach, 'this is accidental only from the perspective of a kind of set of changeless categories of style and of an idea of a complete analysis which would exhaust the work by going down a list' (1961: x). No such checklist exists for the genuinely new, though of course it may be cobbled together on the basis of what already exists and with respect to what appears different in the new. Something like this has happened with postmodernism, with the effect that its style is less understood for itself than its failure to somehow be properly modernist is bemoaned. In actuality, the new, if it is really new, bursts forth unheralded, leaving us to race after it and try to learn its constitutive criteria on the run. Now, the essential proposition that follows on from this, is that the new work generates its own categories; then, 'once the new thing is present, it is bound to give its qualification for being there' (Jameson 1961: x).

'Understanding' is thus synonymous with a form of cultural analysis that is not merely sensitive and alert to the new, but open enough not to have be constantly trying to accommodate it within a basically too rigid framework. Instead of trying to capture changes in culture as a new combination of old elements, what de Certeau aims at delivering is a specification of 'culture' as a force of semanticisation (1997a: 21). At its best, the new form of the analysis will be able to adapt in response to the shifts occurring on the cultural plane at the level of content: for instance, in the midst of a 'cultural revolution' it would not continue to harp on about established values nor cling to a model of progress as though historiography had no other tropes to play, nor alternative forms to utilise, but would try to let the events speak for themselves as a form and hear whatever it is their perpetrators are struggling to say through their violence, their slogans, their sit-ins, and so forth.[5] In other words, 'understanding' is primarily a language experiment, as Jameson might put it, because articulating events in their own form is by no means straightforward (1961: 67). What is the formal equivalent of a cultural revolution? What phrase could have the same shock value as a barricade, or a Molotov cocktail? What type of exposition could capture adequately the simple rage and the powerful economy of expression of a good, marching slogan? All of these questions (and many more, as well, of course) had to be faced and worked through by the commentators of the 'Events' of May 1968, de Certeau insisted, if they were not to fall into the trap of judging them by the old criteria through habit, or what amounts to the same thing, a culpably dire lack of an appropriate discourse.[6]

Just as the important novelists of the nineteenth-century, by which I mean those writers who – according to Marxist tradition, at least – had a well-developed social conscience and an alert critical sensibility (Dickens, Stendahl, Dostoevsky, to name some of the more celebrated), had to discover new means of representing class struggle with the advent of the industrial revolution, so the culturally concerned critics of the mid-twentieth-century had to discover the rhetorical means of representing its various cultural revolutions.[7] By the middle part of the twentieth-century, though, for reasons which need to be examined in detail, a profound suspiciousness had come to settle on narrative in all its grander forms, especially that form of it Lukács referred to as realism, the success story of the previous era. Its supremacy had of course already been disputed by the avant-garde writers of the early decades of the twentieth-century, who refused it natural assent. In literary circles, realism was laid to rest altogether by Joyce with the publication in 1922 of his literally shattering piece of experimentation, *Ulysses*. But in historiography these experimentations had little or no immediate effect. Indeed, in the late 1960s, a realism of sorts was still the standard for all history writing, and it was against precisely this model that de Certeau's rhetorical challenge was directed. He was not himself immediately successful in his bid to renovate historiography, and in this respect his commentary on the Events of May 1968 are perhaps best seen as a 'call'.[8]

Heeding this call, *The Possession of Loudun*, published only a couple of years later in 1970, should therefore be read at least as much for its experimental mode of representation as for what it has to say about certain infamous events that occurred in a seventeenth-century, Ursuline convent.[9] And in this later work, which ostensibly returns us to the benighted years 1632–1640, one can certainly still hear echoes of the Events of May 1968, muffled but threatening like the sound of gunfire in the distance. Nowhere is the appalling din of this unresting memory louder than in the book's opening: 'Normally, the uncanny circulates discreetly below street level. But a crisis will suffice to bring it flooding up everywhere from underneath, pushing aside manhole covers, inundating the cellars, then the towns themselves. It always comes as a surprise when the nocturnal erupts into broad daylight' (de Certeau, 1996a: 7). The sound of the present is deliberately pointed up by de Certeau in order to expose as politically-charged what some believe is so obvious as to be comfortably ignored, namely the fact that history begins in the present. Operating on a 'structural' level, his chosen method of 'estrangement' (Brecht's [1964] term for awakening attention to the historical nature of things ordinarily thought of as changeless) is to publish his archival material and his commentary together so as to permit their palpable differences 'to disclose an historical distance' (de Certeau, 1996a: 14). Instead of absorbing the past into its infinitely dilatable present as history texts customarily do, *The Possession of Loudun* uses the past to blast that present apart in such a way as to free it from its habitual posture of a continuum. In this respect, it is decidedly Benjaminesque (particularly as Eagleton characterises it):

> Those who avoid a 'rupture between the nocturnal and the daytime worlds' (Benjamin may well have the dangers of surrealism in mind) bring calamity, since in folding history back into the unconscious, in reducing the present to a mere stuttering repetition of the past, they rob both past and unconscious of their emancipatory force, which is to be always elsewhere. It is only through the radical discontinuity of past and

present, through the space hollowed by their mutual eccentricity, that the former may be brought to bear explosively upon the latter. Any attempt to recuperate the past directly, non-violently, will result only in paralysing complicity with it. (Eagleton, 1981: 43–4)

Such violent rhetoric as 'blasting free' might seem out of place in a description of so peaceful sounding a project as 'understanding'; yet, as Benjamin saw ('blasting free' is his catchcry), violence is oftentimes needed at precisely those moments when peacefulness seems to be reigning supreme because quiescence can often be synonymous with that rank conformism we have come to associate with fascism.

To articulate the past historically does not mean to recognise it 'the way it was really was' (Ranke). It means to seize hold of a memory as it flashes up at a moment of danger. Historical materialism wishes to retain that image of the past which unexpectedly appears to a man singled out by history at a moment of danger. The danger affects both the content of the tradition and its receivers. The same threat hangs over both: that of becoming a tool of the ruling classes. In every era the attempt must be made anew to wrest tradition away from a conformism that is about to overpower it. (Benjamin, 1968: 255)

This, I believe, is how we should understand the above cited injunction that the event should be let to teach us how to cast doubt on mental habits or social reflexes that would lead us to call it meaningless or to forget its significance. Making our analyses a function of the event itself, understanding's key aim, amounts therefore to a blasting free of the seductive inertia of complacency: in the 1960s and 1970s this meant escaping the easygoing clutches of narrative by power of a thoroughgoing formalisation of its properties and its operations.

In de Certeau's work this 'resistance' to narrative – as it might be called because of the enormous investment (in Deleuze and Guattari's [1983] sense of the term) that was put into it, not only by de Certeau, but an entire generation of scholars – was conducted on two levels that I will designate as narrative and metanarrative.[10] In historiography, narrative, in its most basic form, is simply a form of expression, a particular way of organising content whose chief characteristics may be specified in terms of a will to attribute sequence and causation to preselected data ('this leads to that'). The fundamental problem narrative presents at both an ideological and epistemological level can itself be posed in terms of sequence: is narrative what one must uncover, after the fact, that is, after one has patiently scrutinised all the available data; or, does it come first, is it what secretly shapes the archive, and selects the documents? In the former scenario, which reflects the traditional view, the historian believes he or she constructs their narrative as a consequence of research: after much reading, weighing of evidence and sifting of data, they conclude that events must have occurred in 'this' order, due to 'these' factors, with the 'following' meaning, and it is 'this' deduction which constitutes history as such, its truth in other words. This view pretends not to place any premium on the actual telling of a history, or on its specific methods of constructing a history, because to do so would be to admit that it had somehow produced the thing it claims to have discovered like a nugget in the earth, namely, the truth.

> When historians suppose that a past already given is unveiled in their text, they align themselves all the more with the consumer's behaviour. They passively receive objects distributed by producers. (de Certeau, 1988: 72)

The alternative viewpoint is that narrative guides research, even if – or, perhaps especially if – unconsciously, by governing the selection of data through deciding what counts as significant and what does not:

> In history everything begins with the gesture of *setting aside*, of putting together, of transforming certain classified objects into 'documents'. This new cultural distribution is the first task. In reality it consists in *producing* such documents by dint of copying, transcribing, or photographing these objects, simultaneously changing their locus and their status. This gesture consists in 'isolating' a body – as in physics – and 'denaturing' things in order to turn them into parts which will fill the lacunae inside an a priori totality. (de Certeau, 1988: 72–3)

Inasmuch as it emphasises both the actual telling of a history and its specific methods of construction, this viewpoint can be considered something of a return of the repressed: it contradicts the 'truth' of history with the fact of its 'artifice'. Yet, unlike a true return of the repressed, its reappearance does not constitute the ruin of the precious order that is constituted by history today, because history is, above all else, a cultural institution. This is to say that as a form and a practice history is endorsed as the official mode of 'our' society's ideology: it is how 'we' (in the most global sense of the term) fix 'our' place in the greater cosmos and attempt to domesticate time; other societies use myths, some use legends, but 'we' use history. Although the structuralist in de Certeau was able to see myth and legend as analogous to history, it did not prevent him from weighing in against them in favour of history (1988: 44–6).

If de Certeau's critique of historiography was scandalous to some, it was undoubtedly because he exposed more frankly than most of his colleagues would have cared for him to do the sheer professionalism of history.[11] He connected cultural endorsement with institutional support and showed that history as we know it is a product and a function of 'place' – not objective thought, nor a heartfelt desire for the truth.

History, de Certeau argued, 'implies an area of elaboration that peculiar determinations circumscribe: a liberal profession, a position as an observer or a professor, a group of learned people, and so forth. It is therefore ruled by constraints, bound to privileges, and rooted in a particular situation. It is in terms of this place that its methods are established, its topography of interests can be specified, its dossiers and its interrogation of documents are organised' (de Certeau, 1988: 58). We will deal more fully with de Certeau's critique of historiography later: for now suffice it to say his scepticism was by no means nihilistic. As we shall see, he did not aim to destroy history, he merely wanted to awaken our attention to its productive depths. There is no attempt made to paint history as a kind of corruption of an essential innocence or anything like that; on the contrary, the key premise of *The Writing of History* is an affirming one. It posits that production is 'historiography's quasi-universal principle of explanation, since historical research grasps every document as the symptom of whatever produced it' (de Certeau, 1988: 11). The hypothesis that follows, which transposes Marx's economic history onto the discipline of history itself, is that if history does indeed amount to a kind of labour of production, then perhaps its product can be equated with capital (de Certeau, 1988: 13).[12]

In other words, de Certeau uses the very principles of historical thinking and writing to produce his own history of historiography. So, very far from resulting in a turning away from history, de Certeau's critique actually amounts to an affirmation of its most coveted secrets, which, of course, could not occur without those secrets first being revealed as fully as possible. Nowhere does de Certeau reject narrative; indeed, he is critical of Paul Veyne precisely for eschewing narrative history's central operations of the attribution of causation and the delineation of sequence.[13] The only unity left in Veyne's work, de Certeau says, is the historian's pleasure (de Certeau, 1988: 60; 80). Yet, if he is not content to let history dwindle into just another form of discourse analysis (as he unhesitatingly accuses Veyne of doing) and seems to want to preserve narrative as one of history's basic commodities, then what is the purpose behind his exposing of the repressed facts of historical production (de Certeau, 1995a: 314)? I do not believe there is a latent Althusserian desire to uncover false consciousness here, however well such a charge could be made to apply. It would be utterly out of character for one thing, but more to the point, from de Certeau's perspective it would be entirely redundant since accusations in themselves do not advance 'understanding' beyond the point of discovery upon which they are based, which, in this case, is the recognition of the formative influence of narrative. But this shouldn't be taken to mean that de Certeau is somehow unconscious of, or unconcerned by, the ideological ramifications of narrative, only that he prefers to tackle it by means other than a high-minded reproach.

His means were of course semiotic, a fact which periodises his work more effectively than mere dates could by fixing him in a 'generation'. His colleagues included such illustrious semioticians as Benveniste, Ducrot, Greimas, Lacan, Lévi-Strauss and Marin, and while he did not see eye to eye with all of them, all the time, he nevertheless participated in a common project with them, the articulation of the formal operations of culture and its institutions. For de Certeau, this meant fathoming the 'inner form', as it were, of what he was to call the 'historiographic operation'. As will be seen, the working premise in his justly famous study of the 'historiographic operation' was precisely structuralist: it takes the position that historiography can be apprehended as a certain type of linguistic system (Jameson, 1972: vii). His own work should thus be seen as the development of the special kind of sentence needed to present this 'other syntax'. Envisaging history as an operation is the equivalent, de Certeau argues, 'to understanding it as the relation between a *place* (a recruitment, a milieu, a profession or business, etc.), analytic *procedures* (a discipline), and the construction of a *text* (a literature). That would be to admit that it is part of the "reality" with which it deals, and that this reality can be grasped "as a human activity", or "as a practice". From this perspective I would like to show that the historical operation refers to a combination of a social *place*, "scientific" *practices*, and *writing*' (de Certeau, 1988: 57). Today it is this conviction that historiography can be rendered in terms of an algorithm – or to use the structuralist word, a *combinatoire* – which seems the most dated aspect of de Certeau's work. Yet in spite of a wealth of post-structuralist critique, which it would be easy to assume has buried structuralism forever, the insights made available by his deployment of this device continue to prove valid and interesting. Undoubtedly it is the synchronic turn that de Certeau effects which is of lasting interest because of the way it diverts attention from the fantastic projections of the content of history itself onto the rather more stolid impact of the place (its situation) of writing on content.

This critique needs to be read in terms of de Certeau's own style, his own search for an apt critical syntax. I want to suggest that de Certeau's relentless formalisations of history's operations and procedures be treated as a kind of philosophical laying bare of the device; as a way, in other words, of making apparent their gross routinisation by the discipline itself.[14] I use this Russian Formalist term because I believe there are both philosophical and rhetorical (or strategic) issues at stake here: formalisation is at once a means of interrogating a text, a way of revealing its pillars and presuppositions, and an acute form of denaturing, one that excoriates rhetoric with the unpalatable evidence of just how little is really being said. Formalisation is as much a matter of representation as it is an instrument of conceptualisation – not only is it a way of conducting an inquiry, it is also a statement of intent. In the same way that an author's self-consciousness about their style is as much a way of drawing attention to the presence of a stylistic operation in progress as it is an essential aspect of that style – think of Milan Kundera's endless self-reflexive interventions – so the formal component of an analysis is both the product of research and the pretext for a certain type of exposition. In the very least, it is another way of saying there are many more operations besides discursive ones – this is what is meant by the above mentioned claim that philosophy is a kind of language experiment. Another way of putting this would be to say de Certeau turns a certain form of structuralist semiotics (one could make much of the fact that de Certeau was an avid participant in the seminars of both Lacan and Greimas) into his means of 'blasting' history from the continuum constituted by its practitioner's more or less blind acceptance of their discipline's traditional understanding of itself as a purely discursive affair.[15]

This brings us to metanarrative, for it seems fairly clear that what de Certeau hoped to achieve by this laying bare of the device with respect to the small form is some kind of a defamiliarisation or estrangement of the large form. This, as we'll see in a moment, can be read off the strategies he employs to bring about a kind of autocritique (as the Marxists call it) of metanarrative.[16] As the description of it as a large form implies, metanarrative is a kind of totalising device which through power of an overarching story transforms a loosely grouped collection of narratives into a singular statement with an expressive force palpably greater than the sum of the individual narratives combined. What makes it a *meta*narrative, though, is the fact that it is supplementary (to speak like Derrida) to the narratives it reputedly represents. Insofar as it embodies all narratives it is paradoxically both one narrative more and several narratives less: it is that one *extra* narrative that obliterates all the others by taking their place. By a strange twist of logic and fate, famously elucidated by Derrida, the metanarrative reverses the usual pattern of the metonym: instead of the part standing for the whole, which is not then put in evidence (the fetishist's shoe replaces the woman), the whole stands for the parts, which, similarly, are then nowhere to be seen (a history replaces many histories).

Now, even if we go along with the general Derridean proposition, that analogous to writing, there is, behind any one narrative, nothing but more narrative, such that the predominance of the metanarrative can never be made fully secure, we must still grapple with the fact that, ideologically speaking, metanarrative is an index of a kind of meta-subject (an immense, 'one who knows'), or global perspective.[17] The deeper problematic of metanarrative, what distinguishes it in effect from mere narrative, is the fact of its achievement of something like a God's-eye view; the grandeur of the view obtained endows the viewing subject, and this applies to the writer and the reader equally, with a kind of omniscience formerly applicable to Gods only. It is thus something of a double-headed beast, the metanarrative, because the viewpoint it constructs (the so-called 'total' view) is the putatively unimpeachable source of authority of the one who proclaims it; yet, by the same token, it takes a special type of arrogance, some would call it ambition, to actually contemplate the notion that one's own view, no matter how encyclopaedic and encompassing, could in fact be called 'total'. This double articulation is part of the reason 'totalising' methods have been vilified as 'totalitarian', in spite of the fact (or perhaps because of it, given the widespread mistrust of utopia) that most attempts at 'totalisation' have strictly ameliorative aims in mind. For instance, Jameson's (1994: 70) use of totalisation is directed at rendering visible the being of capital in such a way as to make it felt for the restrictive force it is with the hope of making it possible for people to envision change once again.

On another level, which we might term 'existential' to differentiate it from the basically emotional level we've just looked at, totalisation excites such a strong response because, to pick up on a remark made by Max Weber in *The Sociology of Religion*, it gets at the heart of one of our most fundamental existential dilemmas: 'The conflict between empirical reality and this conception of the world as a meaningful totality, which is based on a religious postulate, produces the strongest tensions in man's inner life as well as in his external relationship to the world' (Weber, 1963: 59). It is, in other words, the unembarrassed assertion of a cosmology that causes the greatest amount of trouble for would-be totalisers because it invites conflict on two fronts, which, to use de Certeau's own preferred discursive framework (Lacan's) we may designate as the imaginary and the symbolic. Every cosmology is something of a wound to the narcissism of the ego because it implies that the world has both meaning and existence irrespective of it; it therefore contradicts the cherished solipsism of the imaginary which sees itself as the centre and source of all meaning. By the same token, the cosmology also conflicts with the subject's sense of their place in the world by redefining the essential hierarchies of that world, its symbolic order in other words. Thus, to pick up the same example once more, Jameson's utopian cosmology, crudely put, foregrounds the collective at the expense of the individual, and favours unity over difference, all of which traits, as he himself illustrates, contradict the presently dominant capitalist cosmology (Jameson, 1994: 65).[18]

Now, I want to suggest that the assertion of a cosmology – my codeword for any form of a totalising model or metanarrative, but we might just as well have used Jameson's own term, borrowed from

Deleuze and Guattari, namely 'transcoding', although I don't think it captures the double-edged tension Weber speaks of so well as 'cosmology' – must suffer the same two basic 'accusations' which, according to Jameson (1988b: viii), the assertion of all utopias endure. Initially it will be a case of reading back into Jameson his own insights in order to explain some of the hostility his ideas have been subject to. But, as will soon be seen, the very things Jameson says utopias must guard against are precisely the weapons de Certeau employs against them. The first accusation, then, which pertains to the symbolic, stems from a fear of something we might call a mirage because of the way it turns on the issue of authenticity. If one can already articulate the shape and flavour of what a better future would look like, then, insofar as its expression must issue from a present symbolic order 'the suspicion arises that it may not really express freedom after all but only repetition' (Jameson, 1994: 56). The second charge, pertaining to the imaginary, derives from a fear of projection: the worry, in other words, that the open future one dreams of is – unbeknownst to you or anyone else – always already contaminated by your 'own deformed and repressed social habits' (Jameson, 1994: 56).[19] Utopia can thus be dismissed as a mirage because no matter how much it shimmers it is not truly futuristic, but – in much the same way that history is – inherently *of* the present; and it can be rejected for being, finally, too personal.

In both cases, the nucleus of the charge bears a family resemblance (without necessarily being family) to false consciousness because it is their potentially self-deceiving qualities that are being picked-up on. This, for de Certeau, is the fundamental problem of metanarrative. The fact that de Certeau couches his own self-reflexive meditations on the problem and possibility of 'totalisation' in libidinal terms is a strong indicator that what concerns him most is the inmost will, desire. 'To what erotics of knowledge does the ecstasy of reading such a cosmos belong? Having taken a voluptuous pleasure in it, I wonder what is the source of this pleasure of "seeing the whole", of looking down on, totalising the most immoderate of human texts' (de Certeau, 1984: 92). It is doubtless the presence of such exacting self-inspections as this, that has prompted certain of de Certeau's commentators (notably his former collaborator Luce Giard [1998a: xxii]) to suggest that an Ignation inspiration is to be detected throughout his work. But, be that as it may, what is important here is the fact that de Certeau does not make the leap one might anticipate would follow such a 'rationalist' excoriation of the libido as we've just encountered; he does not, in other words, call for a renewal of objectivity via the suppression the bodily. On the contrary, he identifies the desire to be aloft the world as a problematic desire to escape the body: elevation, he says, 'transforms the bewitching world by which one was "possessed" into a text that lies before one's eyes. It allows one to read it, to be a solar Eye, looking down like a god. The exaltation of a scopic and gnostic drive: the fiction of knowledge is related to this lust to be a viewpoint and nothing more' (de Certeau, 1984: 92).

So right where one expects a call for a more finely chiselled form of objectivity, de Certeau instead asks for a more earthly quality of subjectivity, one that acknowledges the banal lusting that inheres in all searches for knowledge. In effect, he turns the metanarrative, at once the instrument and figure of all such attempts at knowing, into a 'desiring-machine' (Deleuze and Guattari, 1983). By associating 'totalised knowledge' with 'libidinal satisfaction', in the way he does, de Certeau turns the former into a function of the latter and thereby discredits it as a self-gratifying fiction, which we are encouraged to interpret as self-deluding. De Certeau's critiques of early European anthropologists Léry, Lafitau and Montaigne (1988: 209–24; 1980b; 1986: 67–79), make this point especially well. Metanarrative is neutralised by de Certeau with the most powerful critical weapon available: the guilt of self-pleasure, the wilful self-deception of autoerotism. To even want to 'see the whole' is – through an insistent repetition of the adjective 'voyeuristic' – made to seem, right from the outset, somehow perverted and dirty. ('For lack of *doing* something, one *looks on*' [de Certeau, 1997b: 18].) But the fiction of 'seeing the whole' is not really despised by de Certeau so much as scorned for being an impoverished compensation for true knowledge. This is brought home to us when, in search of his own analogy to characterise the functionally inverted metonymy of the metanarrative Derrida terms supplementation, de Certeau draws on the supposed built-in, philosophical (if not actual) disappointment (already identified by Barthes) of the striptease.[20]

The analogy seems to be that the search for the conceptual bare-all of metanarrative is ultimately counter-productive because it flings away the very things that give it significance.[21] And one can readily imagine that this argument could be extended, along the lines of a compulsion to repeat, to cast almost all academic inquiry in a queer yellow light of untold compensatory behaviour. The logic of the metanarrative, which he says is becoming evident everywhere, is as self-defeating as that of the striptease, de Certeau argues, because when the stripper bares her body to reveal her 'all' the spectator is similarly dispossessed as she of the one thing that gives meaning to the moment, namely her clothes, which, to speak like Heidegger, are thrown into being, but also into non-being as well, as they are cast aside (1997b: 18). The stripper's clothes are thus figures of all that academic inquiry into the everyday wilfully ignores, namely, the ultra-mundane, ordinary, repetitive and dull words and gestures of similarly ordinary folk going about the boring business of their daily lives. What de Certeau is satirising, of course, is the fantasy that if you strip all this ordinariness away some kind of startling body of truth will be found.[22] In reality, there is nothing else besides the mundane, it is that which gives the everyday its thickness. By the same token, and this was Barthes' point, the stripper's clothes do not merely cloak her nudity, they contradict it in such a way as to give it meaning (a similar logic can be seen in Heidegger's notion of veiling). De Certeau's objection to totalising models, in short, is that they arrive at their functional pictures of society at the expense of the very people who inhabit it.

> The panorama-city is a 'theoretical' (that is, visual) simulacrum, in short a picture, whose condition of possibility is an oblivion and a misunderstanding of practices. The voyeur-god created by the fiction, who, like Schreber's God, knows only cadavers, must disentangle himself from the murky intertwining daily behaviours and make himself alien to them. (de Certeau, 1984: 93)

By eroticising the very aim of certain types of intellectual endeavour, an eroticisation that follows on more or less naturally from the fact that today intellectual work is increasingly commodified, de Certeau is able to push them into a none too easily eluded position of seeming utterly self-serving, not to mention foolishly beguiled by their very own blandishments, such that any credibility these methods might have had is completely destroyed.[23] If 'totalisation' is merely the satisfaction of the somewhat eerie desire to become a mere cipher, a bodiless point of view, then it is rather simply dismissed as lunatic, albeit interestingly so. In classic Freudian fashion, then, de Certeau teaches us to be suspicious of the hidden operations of desire that lurk beneath and behind every surface and every gesture. Unlike Freud, though, who maintained that through science one could always rise above the irrationalities of the body, de Certeau did not see that things could be otherwise. So while it may seem reactionary to base a critical scepticism on the secret machinations of desire it is in fact very close to the work of those avant-garde prophets of desiring, Deleuze and Guattari, whose liberation rhetoric probably appears antithetical to de Certeau's. If one substitutes desiring-machine for metanarrative, as I've suggested above, the congruence between Deleuze and Guattari and de Certeau will be somewhat clearer; for, in effect, what this substitution implies is that metanarratives are not 'above' the bodily, as though an idea could elevate itself into the ether by sheer will, but, on the contrary, part and parcel of the way the body functions.

What is especially interesting about this particular move of de Certeau's is the fact that it inverts the accepted image of narrative as personal and metanarrative as collective. For, as we've already seen, narrative insofar as it is a formalisation is in fact *im*personal, while as we're seeing here, metanarrative, because of its self-gratifying effects of comprehensiveness and closure is exceedingly personal. If there is a faint trace of anti-intellectualism here, then it is directed at the blind arrogance of a scholar who would dare presume their own vision of the world is a complete picture. It should also be said, that this pointing-up of the libidinal underside of metanarrative is consistent with at least some of the more essential aspects of a Weberian mode of analysis, though in general de Certeau does not invest quite so much interest in class as Weber does. That being said, de Certeau, as Weber does, clearly sees the intellectual's interest in metanarrative as deeply personal, and not socially motivated as some of its utopian adherents would claim: 'The salvation sought by the intellectual is always based on inner need, and hence it is at once more remote from life, more theoretical and more systematic than salvation from external distress, the quest for which is characteristic of nonprivileged classes' (Weber, 1963: 124–5). The idea that revolutions can be lead from the top, as it were, is for any intellectual an obviously appealing fantasy (think of T.S. Eliot), but as numerous Marxist critics, among others, have pointed out, it is a wish destined never to come true because the sheer, high-minded elitism of the notion is repellent to the very people needed for its success: it cannot hope for popular support because it does not arise from the popular imagination, nor stem from problems found in the everyday.[24] To which we must add de Certeau's (1986: 126–31) own suspicions concerning the use of 'popular', which he generally regarded as a sleight of hand by which an intellectual got to speak in the place of the people by pretending to speak for them.

In other words, de Certeau does not merely haul critical theory over the coals for not being self-reflexive enough, he in fact demands its reinvention. By illustrating that desire, the body, the lived reality concepts are supposed to inform us about cannot simply be injected into thought as so much content, he calls for a new form of analysis to be found which is as vibrant and fungible as everyday life is at street level.[25] To live up to this ambition, though, it would have to be a mode of analysis that is as coherent and contradictory, as coherently contradictory or contradictorily coherent, as is the everyday itself. And we will have occasion to see whether in fact de Certeau achieves this aim in his own investigations into the nature of the everyday. The real difficulty, however, is not coming up with such a model, although that is not to say it is easy, but in finding a way of thwarting the seemingly inevitable recuperation of it by the incredibly resilient forces of metanarrative. Because metanarrative is, in our time at least, the most satisfying intellectual form, and by this I do mean precisely libidinally gratifying, it is not something we can easily give up. Even if the satisfactions they used to afford are on the wane, as perhaps Lyotard's (1984: xxiv) epochal claim that in postmodernity metanarratives are increasingly subject to incredulity may be interpreted, that does not mean that they have died out altogether, only that a greater sophistication is expected of them. As Freud has taught us, we almost never relinquish sources of pleasure, no matter how peculiar, we simply disguise them in more and more elaborate ways.

This means, as the organisation of de Certeau's later books suggests, that so entrenched a habit as metanarrative cannot simply be replaced by an alternative strategy, as no cosmology can simply be replaced by another; it has to be actively broken up and prevented from returning. In these later works, particularly *The Writing of History* and *Mystic Fable*, de Certeau carries the fight against metanarrative to its logical end: he not only refuses to offer a metanarrative, he constructs his books in such a way as to inhibit its resurrection as well. Where one would normally expect to encounter the first lineaments of a metanarrative (obeying that logic which Hegel – and after him Derrida [1981: 7–12] – pointed up as paradoxically placing the conclusion before the exposition), namely in the preface or introduction, de Certeau substitutes the systematic explanation of a position, or place. Instead of pretending that his work is somehow the embodiment of time itself, its transfiguration into text in other words, as the realist, or linear causal, conception of historiographic metanarrative would have it, he offers his work as a 'place' where a limited number of historiographic operations occur (de Certeau, 1988: xxvi; 1992: 3). 'Place', quite purposefully, does not have the same 'authority' as metanarrative, meaning, the same ability to lull disbelief and foster adherence, because it foregrounds its own conditions of possibility and construction, something no doctrine can do and still hope to inspire faith (Weber, 1963: 192).

Yet, as de Certeau recognises, thwarting metanarrative on this one level alone is not enough to prevent its restitution because the effect of this breaking up of the grand projection of the metanarrative is the displacement onto the author of all its ideological power. Where once it was metanarrative that led to the construction of a notion of a meta-subject, today the absence of metanarrative is compensated by the presumption of a meta-subject, the author: a unity of consciousness as the source of the text is substituted for the destroyed unity of vision once projected by texts.[26] It is against this default form of metanarrative that de Certeau's laying bare of the device of narrative as a formal procedure coupled with his pointing-up of the libidinal impulses underpinning historiography in general is working its hardest to estrange. What his strategy of emphasising the fact that history is a profession, a form of labour in other words, carried out by real men and women, with the full complement of idiosyncrasies and foibles, effectively does is reduce the meta-subject to properly mortal proportions.[27] Thus, it is always with great modesty that de Certeau enacts his texts.[28] De Certeau's figuration of this is literally an image of descent, but it should not be taken literally.[29] His fabled journey from the top of the World Trade Centre in New York down to the street, with all its bump and grind, is a symbolic one, the message being that a God's-eye view is God's alone (de Certeau, 1984: 92–3).

It should be clear from the foregoing, that de Certeau does not champion the view 'down below' (which would merely substitute one type of metanarrative for another), as some (Soja, 1996: 313–14) have suggested. But that still leaves open the question of what exactly de Certeau offers in the place of metanarrative? The answer to this question, which we see revealed at the conclusion of the fable of his visit to the World Trade Centre in New York, is a logic of practices. When totalising notions of the order I have referred to here as metanarratives, such as the 'city', or even 'the popular', have been thoroughly discredited, when, in effect, the distortions of their prospective visions (as de Certeau calls it, his anti-utopianism surfacing once more) have been corrected, then, the real (in contrast to the imaginary and symbolic realms that cultural theory has hitherto contented itself with) is finally exposed. For de Certeau there is a dialectical relation between what constitutes the real and what he sees as unreal, or mere projection, namely metanarrative. The former contradicts the latter by mocking its attempts at transparency with its own thick opacity: 'Escaping the imaginary totalisations produced by the eye, the everyday has a certain strangeness that does not surface, or whose surface is only its upper limit, outlining itself against the visible' (de Certeau, 1984: 93). Yet, however much the point might be laboured, and it must be admitted that de Certeau does go to some lengths to specify as vividly and fully as possible the elusiveness of his topic, the primary problem is not, as one might expect, that the everyday is impossible to see, for that would effectively render moot de Certeau's entire project, but rather that it is impossible to represent.

Although it is perhaps to be expected, at least according to its well-known Lacanian inscription as that which resists transfiguration, de Certeau does not, as I might just now have made it seem, treat the real as unpresentable by definition. Again, that would defeat his often stated purpose of bringing to light the logic of the practices of everyday life in all their filigreed glory, which is what, finally, we come to realise 'understanding' means. If, as Blanchot insists, the everyday truly was that which escapes then de Certeau would not have a project, or if he did, it would be every bit as delusory and worthless as the ones he critiques.[30] Indeed, de Certeau opens the second volume of *The Practice of Everyday Life*, a work he directed rather than wrote, with what amounts to a war cry concerning the imperceptibility of his topic. 'It's not all that invisible' (de Certeau, 1998: 3) he says, contra Paul Leuilliot. This is why de Certeau's critiques of metanarrative are couched in the careful terms they are: he does not chastise metanarrative for chasing after the impossible, like some mad admirer of Don Quixote; he criticises it for failing in its bid to represent the real.

The fine point of distinction that needs to be underscored here is that while in de Certeau's view the everyday contradicts the various projections of the metanarrative type (the city, the panopticon and so on), it should not therefore be construed as the 'negative' term in a dialectical equation, however much it might feel like a descent into the dark night, because insofar as it 'deconstructs' metanarrative it actually amounts to a 'negation of the negation'.[31]

> It is true that the operations of walking can be traced on city maps in such a way as to transcribe their paths (here well-trodden, there very faint) and their trajectories (going this way and not that). But these thick or thin curves only refer, like words, to the absence of what has passed by. Surveys of routes miss what was: the act itself of passing by. The operation of walking, wandering, or 'window shopping', that is, the activity of passers-by, is transformed into points that draw a totalising and reversible line on the map. They allow us to grasp only a relic set in the nowhen of a surface of projection. Itself visible, it has the effect of making invisible the operations that made it possible. (de Certeau, 1984: 97)

The everyday is not invisible by definition: it is *made* so by the clumsy attempts to represent it. A sure way, then, of illuminating the everyday is to dispose of the multitude of apparatuses that one way or another are today endeavouring to articulate the everyday 'as a whole'. This constitutes, as we have seen, de Certeau's first line of attack, or what he refers to as the necessary 'negative' work of setting aside certain of the predominant modes of inquiry within the broad field of cultural inquiry (1984: xii). It amounts to insisting that the everyday *is* there, only we're too blind to see it, or else (for a variety of ideological reasons, ranging from the basically well-intended to the unambiguously malicious) have allowed ourselves to be blinded. This argument is made especially vividly in 'The Beauty of the Dead' (de Certeau, 1986), which illustrates the obstinate persistence of an idea current in the middle of last century that popular culture needs 'saving'. The real problem, though, as this article illustrates, is that most of the available modes for articulating the everyday, thanks largely to the pretence to scientificity, are totally inadequate to the task.[32] As such, a positive task ensues the negative task: clearing away the blinkers is not sufficient in and of itself to attain the clarity of vision de Certeau desires, one must conceive of a new conceptual discourse as well. Thus, as we shall see more fully in a later chapter, the logic of practices de Certeau proposes is a language experiment in the form of a description of the everyday. What 'understanding' entails, in effect, is the generation of a new type of critical syntax, or force of semanticisation.

As is the case with the scientific methods referred to already, the primary fault de Certeau finds with the vast majority of the 'older'

critical syntaxes (sociology, psychology and anthropology) is their
apparent inability to deal with culture as it lives and breathes, much less
enunciate it. For the most part, he finds that cultural analysis treats
culture as a static, unliving thing, and, what is worse, seems to feel no
qualms at all in 'killing' culture, as though, in the end, cultural analysis
is really just another way of saying taxidermy or vivisection.[33] Real,
living and breathing, culture will thus always be heterogeneous to these
rigid attempts to depict it. But, as we've seen, it is no help at all to
suppose that culture is permanently elsewhere because that is simply to
move from the dead to the ghostly. De Certeau's approach is very
different. His gambit is to suppose that culture is at bottom logical,
which is not quite the same thing as rational (Weber), but it does share
the implication that culture is fundamentally a calculating activity, not a
dumb, unconscious one (Freud, Bourdieu). By further supposing that
this logic might be found in nature itself he makes logic into a kind of
living algorithm, like DNA, instead of a dead metaphor as most types of
formalisation result in. What we must ask, therefore, is what kind of a
solution to the particular problems of representation 'living culture'
poses is a logic of practices? Before we can take up this question we
must first of all pass by way of de Certeau's critique of historiography
because it is there in inverted form that we hear the first rumblings of
this need to reconcile a live culture with a dead discourse. History poses
the problem of accommodating death within the living in such a way as
to make us realise that insofar as any representation of 'living culture'
proves itself unable to accommodate death its discourse is privative.
Ultimately, it is this privation of the living that de Certeau's logic of
practices hopes to overcome – the move to logic should be read as an
attempt to find an immanent ground capable of thinking death within
life.

Notes

[1] A shorter version of this chapter previously appeared in *Paragraph*
22 (2): 133–45.

[2] 'I can't help but dream about a kind of criticism that would try not
to judge but to bring an oeuvre, a book, a sentence, an idea to life; it would
light fires, watch the grass grow, listen to the wind, and catch the sea foam in
the breeze and scatter it' (Foucault, 1997: 323).

[3] 'Something that had been tacit began to stir, something that
invalidates the mental hardware built for stability. Its instruments were also
part of what shifted, went awry. They referred to something *unthinkable*, which,
last May, was unveiled while being contested: values taken to be self-evident;
social exchanges, the progress of which was enough to define their success;
commodities, the possession of which represented happiness' (de Certeau,
1997a: 4).

[4] De Certeau (1997a: 22) explicitly rejects both psychological and sociological methods on these grounds.

[5] It is worth noting here that de Certeau himself resists using the phrase 'cultural revolution' to describe the 'Events' of May 1968, dismissing it from consideration as too problematic (1997a: 13). I use 'cultural revolution' here in the sense Jameson (1988b: 174) does, to describe a tumultuous period in history when different modes of production visibly coexist, and do so in an agitated tension with one another. On this view, 'cultural revolution' operates as a mediating device in much the same way that 'haunting' does, it presupposes that the old and the new need time to work out a living arrangement, and that in the meantime they're bound to rub one another the wrong way.

[6] The main problem, as de Certeau saw it, was the one 'posed by the disparity between a fundamental experience and the deficit of its language, between the "positivity" of something lived and the "negativity" of an expression that, in the form of a refusal, resembles more the symptom than the elaboration of the reality being designated' (de Certeau, 1997a: 15).

[7] 'It might be argued, for example, that in an earlier stage of industrial capitalist accumulation, where the dominant ideological experience was one of fragmentation and nuclearity, literary realism fulfilled a progressive role in revealing covert interconnections – in demonstrating, in short, the power and character of something like a system. It might then be argued that, once that system was indeed fleshed within ideological experience – once industrial capitalism had passed into its monopoly forms – modernism in art arrived upon the agenda as a resistance to precisely all that, exploiting the fragment, the private and the unspeakable, the agonised and irreducible moment, as the lone necessary negation of the apparently "monolithic" society it confronted' (Eagleton, 1981: 89–90).

[8] A similar 'call' is to be found in Jameson's work, for similar reasons. As he puts it, 'What is blurred, left out, what does not compute or is "inexpressible", in this or that theoretical language may ... be a more damaging indictment of the "theory" in question than traditional ontological or metaphysical critiques' (Jameson, 1988b: ix).

[9] Ken Russell's film *Devils* and Huxley's book *The Devils of Loudun* are by this measure 'traditional' and even 'realist'.

[10] For an explanation of 'investment' see Deleuze and Guattari, 1983: 9.

[11] For a report on de Certeau's scandalising of his history colleagues see: Giard, 1998a: xiv–xv; Chartier, 1997: 40.

[12] In this respect, *The Writing of History* is remarkably congruent to Deleuze and Guattari's *Anti-Oedipus*, which is similarly predicated by the Marxian notion of production (1983: 4).

[13] Roger Chartier (1997: 42) goes so far as to read de Certeau's landmark article, 'The Historiographic Operation' as, in part, a reply to Veyne. For a comparative analysis of the different conceptions of history offered by de Certeau and Veyne, see Le Goff, 1992: 101–6.

[14] As Barthes rather wittily put it, 'a little formalism turns one away from History, but ... a lot brings one back' (1972: 120).

[15] For this biographical tidbit see Giard, 1998a: xv.

[16] Autocritique, or self-critique, as Deleuze and Guattari (1983: 311) see it, goes beyond what they call the pious destructions of the Hegelians to a point which reveals itself as the objective being of desire.

[17] 'What we have tried to show by following the guiding line of the "dangerous supplement", is that in what one calls the real life of these existences "of flesh and bone", beyond and behind what one believes can be circumscribed as Rousseau's text, there has never been anything but writing; there have never been anything but supplements, substitutive significations which could only come forth in a chain of differential references, the "real" supervening, and being added only while taking on meaning from a trace and from an invocation of the supplement, etc.' (Derrida, 1974: 158–9).

[18] By the same token, as de Certeau (1988: 28) points out, we might also have used Weber's *Weltanschauung*, or Kuhn's 'paradigm', or even Lovejoy's 'unit idea'.

[19] See also my (Buchanan, 1998a) extended discussion of Jameson's use of the concept of utopia.

[20] 'Striptease – at least Parisian striptease – is based on a contradiction: Woman is desexualised at the very moment when she is stripped naked' (Barthes, 1972: 91).

[21] It needs to be added, though, that de Certeau's conception of the striptease and its textual cousin pornography, is exceedingly ascetic. He treats them both as affronts to metaphysics, and not cultural practices as his own precepts would seem to dictate. To say that pornography calls for no 'practice' on behalf of its user seems to me to miss the point of pornography, it renders its quite practical applications oddly inert, thus making it seem nearer to the very form de Certeau (1997b: 18) reproaches it for not being, namely art.

[22] 'The confession of the heart and, in a more radical but (paradoxically) more symbolic way, the undressing of the body function as the allegory of a quest for pleasure, for communion, or for reality. It is a demystification even if it still retains the form of a myth. The search for a truth is thus "represented"' (de Certeau, 1997b: 22).

[23] On the commodification of intellectual work, see de Certeau, 1997b: 60; on the eroticisation of commodities, see de Certeau, 1997b: 21.

[24] As Eagleton, characteristically acerbicly, puts it: 'Eliot's erudite primitivism, his belief that if the lower classes were grabbed by their visceral regions then their minds would follow, foundered on the minor difficulty that they didn't read his poetry – something that his notoriously olympian public bearing effectively conceded in advance' (1981: 111).

[25] 'The everyday is not at home in our dwelling places; it is not in offices or churches any more than in libraries or museums. If it is anywhere, it is in the street' (Blanchot, 1993: 242).

[26] As Foucault has shown (1977: 124–38), the 'author-function' is as effective a means of totalising as metanarrative.

[27] 'In spite of the contradictory ideologies that may accompany it, the setting-aside of the subject-object relation or of the discourse-object relation is the abstraction that generates an illusion of "authorship". It removes the traces of belonging to a network – traces that always compromise the author's rights' (de Certeau, 1984: 44).

[28] For example, in the opening of *Mystic Fable* de Certeau writes: 'In explicating the conditions of production of this text, I desire from the outset to strip this log of my textual peregrinations of the prestige (in this case they would be brazenly immodest, even obscene) of being taken for a discourse accredited by a presence, authorised to speak in its name, or presumed privy to an insider's knowledge' (de Certeau, 1992: 1).

[29] Although it is obviously presented as a fable, that is, an instructive story whose purpose is to preface – or, enact by other means – a certain pedagogic point, it is still prone to misreadings of an overly literal type, as indeed all figurative writing is. In one instance, at least, this has resulted in the nonsensical impression that de Certeau's 'theory recognises two classes only' (Pickering and Kehde, 1998: 343).

[30] 'Whatever its other aspects, the everyday has this essential trait: it allows no hold. It escapes' (Blanchot, 1993: 239).

[31] 'When one examines this fleeting and permanent reality carefully, one has the impression of exploring the night-side of societies, a night longer than their day, a dark sea from which the successive institutions emerge, a maritime immensity on which socioeconomic and political structures appear as ephemeral islands' (de Certeau, 1984: 41).

[32] 'The question, then, is not one of ideologies, or of options, but that of the relations of an object and its associated scientific methods to the society that sanctions them. And if the procedures of science are not innocent, if their objectives depend on a political structure, then the discourse of science itself should acknowledge the function allotted it by society: to conceal what it claims to show. What this means is that a simple improvement in methods, or a reversal of conviction, will not change what that scientific operation does to popular culture' (de Certeau, 1986: 121).

[33] By the same token, this 'murder' is neither admitted, nor otherwise expressed anywhere in the resulting 'scientific' discourse (de Certeau, 1986: 128).

3. Meta-historiography

As a mirror of the 'doing' which defines a society today, historical discourse is its representation and its underside.

Michel de Certeau, *The Writing of History*

In one of her numerous biographical pieces on de Certeau, Luce Giard informs us that de Certeau read and re-read Marx's *The Eighteenth Brumaire of Louis Bonaparte*. She then makes the rather stunning admission that she cannot fathom why this should have been so (Giard, 1997a: xii). Yet even a cursory glance at that work would make its appeal to de Certeau obvious: like Marx, he wondered why the dead cannot be let to bury the dead. Why do we resort to myths and ghosts so readily? Historians, de Certeau shows, have, since Michelet at least, made it their primary business to assuage the dead, to find the discursive means of putting them to rest, finally, all while pretending it was somebody else who had in fact caused them to be disturbed in the first place. Like the proverbial sufferer of Munchausen's syndrome by proxy, historians allow that the dead have a voice only so they can quieten it (de Certeau, 1988: 2). Understood from the point of view of its function in society, history has to be seen as a kind of cultural machine for easing the anxiety we all seem to feel in the face of death, in the West at least. For what it consists in, for the most part, is a raising of the spectre of our own inevitable demise within a memorial framework that makes it appear we'll live for ever after all. A labour of and against death, de Certeau called it (1988: 5).

De Certeau's take on history might well be described as meta-historiographical, in the sense of Jameson's (1988a) metacommentary I mean not White's (1973) metahistory, because rather than ask what type of discourse history is, as White does, it begins with the dialectical question (Jameson's) of what cultural need does history fulfil? It is this sort of question that leads de Certeau to conclude, as I've already signalled, that history is primarily a discursive working-through of a kind of cultural mourning. To see history as a labour of and against death is to wonder why we should be so concerned to settle our accounts with the past, why in other words we seem to *need* history? To put it another way, it amounts to wondering if the past isn't somehow culturally cathected. Pursuing this psychoanalytic point a little further, we start to wonder whether there is something innately peculiar about the past which explains our 'hysterical' reaction to it. But as soon as you ask that, you must also ask what truly counts as the past. At that point, as de Certeau shows, you discover that it is a product of an equally tenuous present: it is literally a phantasm. That is, a repressed projection born of the two wounds to the ego inflicted by the inevitability of death, namely the unacceptable fact that what is dead is indeed lost for ever and that there is nothing we can do to stave it off. In the next chapter we will revisit this same point from a completely different angle – philosophy rather than history – in an effort to understand de Certeau's unfinished heterological project.

History, de Certeau argues, posits death in order to deny it. The face of death is always that of the Other, both in its Lacanian inflection as that which is insistently lacking and in its Levinasian sense as that which judges us: 'The other is the phantasm of historiography, the object that it seeks, honours and buries' (de Certeau, 1988: 2). Although psychoanalysis (in both its Freudian and Lacanian modes) is an obvious inspiration for de Certeau, one should not thereby discount the influence of other intellectual systems such as semiotics, particularly in its more structuralist phase (for example, the early Barthes, Greimas and Marin). Of course, if anything can be made of de Certeau's assiduous attendance of Lacan's seminars, then we should expect to find the two modes of discourse working in tandem, and that, I want to argue, is exactly what we do find. Ultimately, though, what makes de Certeau's perspective on historiography so remarkable is the fresh view of it he is able to obtain by treating the field of historical discourse as a whole in the same way that, on its own account, it treats its predecessors myth and tradition, that is, as a socially productive process whose function cannot be simply read off its products (1988: 45). History's function in society is not determinable by content analysis alone; it is a very particular mode of communication, whose rules of production and conditions of possibility only become visible when sufficient critical distance *á la* Brecht (1964) is attained to see them in an historical light too.

The precedent for this type of discourse analysis is to be found in the early work of Barthes, especially his inquiry into myth, but also, obviously enough, in his work on Michelet. I am referring here to what I take to be the deep structure of their respective analyses, for it is clear enough that de Certeau does not agree with Barthes in every respect when it comes to the analysis of what in the structuralist vernacular of the time was called textuality. In fact, at times, they could not be further apart. To de Certeau's way of thinking the problem with Barthes' take on history is twofold: on the one hand, he too readily elides the distinction between histories and History (he takes together the work of Herodotus, Machiavelli, Bossuet and Michelet in a single sweep by assuming they're homologous); on the other hand, he treats History itself as just another form of an achieved signified. History, as such, does not survive Barthes because he demolishes both its specificity and its generality (de Certeau, 1988: 41–5). In practice, Barthes' method could at times overreach itself and like an unregulated blow torch burn a little too brightly, thus destroying instead of synthesising the materials it came into contact with. But that does not mean as tool his method did not have its uses.

Barthes inaugurated a type of discourse analysis which looked first to the social effect of a discourse (which he always took to be a systemic manipulation of the meaning potential of language), and then asked how it was able to achieve it. How, in other words, given its apparently limitless meaning-potential, was it able to inhibit potential counter readings? His justly famous decoding of pasta and laundry detergent advertisements took the form, then, of detecting at the level of the text the preferred reading of their images and seeing how the alternatives were suppressed (Barthes, 1977: 32–51; 1972: 40–2). Similarly, de Certeau's analyses of historiography probe the construction of preferred readings and interest themselves in what gets purposefully forgotten. By deep structure, then, I really mean the seismic shift in perspective that enables Barthes to apprehend myth – and de Certeau to grasp history – as an exteriority, which in turn permits these discourses to be seen as peculiar types of cultural machines. This, I believe, is how we should interpret de Certeau's claim that history has become our myth: history and myth are not the same thing, nor do they function in the same way, but from a diachronic perspective it can be said that history now performs the role that used to belong to myth.[1]

The role a discourse plays can best be seen from the reader's or viewer's point of view (not the author's, in other words).[2] Myth, Barthes argued, turns history into nature: 'Entrusted with "glossing over" an intentional concept, myth encounters nothing but betrayal in language, for language can only obliterate the concept if it hides it, or unmask it if it formulates it. The elaboration of a second-order semiological system will enable myth to escape this dilemma: driven to having either to unveil or to liquidate the concept, it will *naturalise* it' (Barthes, 1972: 140). Looking at myth from the reader's point of view means identifying all those moments in a reading of a text when the speculative and critical faculties we would usually put into effect in order to ascertain meaning are somehow neutralised, or otherwise rendered inoperative, by power of their evident redundancy – at such points there is no need to ask 'what does it mean?' because the meaning is patent. 'Myth does not deny things, on the contrary, its function is to talk about them; simply, it purifies them, it makes them innocent, it gives them a natural and eternal justification, it gives them a clarity which is not that of an explanation but that of a statement of fact' (Barthes, 1972: 156). This is not an analysis of style, or ideological content, it is an interrogation of an effect that a certain kind of textuality has within a certain kind of world-system.

What Barthes omits to say, however, is that we have to be prepared for these myth-effects in very deliberate ways or else we will not be affected by them, which is where psychoanalysis comes into its own. This is an anthropological extension of Norman Holland's point, noted by Jameson (1994: 175), that literary texts will not yield myth-effects unless they are primed to do so in advance. The larger part of de Certeau's account of historiography has to do with an explanation of precisely this: the means by which we are culturally primed, so to speak, for history effects. Thus we come to what I think is the crucial pivot-point in de Certeau's analysis of historiography, the claim that history is an instrument of culture, not merely its record: 'History finally refers to a "making", a "doing", which is not only its own ("making history"), but also that of the society which specifies a certain scientific production. If it allows a common way of operating to find its own technical language, it refers to this social praxis as what allows a production of texts organised around a new intelligibility of the past' (de Certeau, 1988: 47). History, in other words, would not exist without a prior cultural need. It is the job of historiography, as we shall see, to at once fulfil this need and repress any evidence of it (hence de Certeau's recourse to psychoanalysis).[3]

What I have wanted to signal in the foregoing is the fact that de Certeau does not treat the actual writing of history in the same way as the production of the concept. Yet the former can only be understood in the context of the latter. The dialectic here, between a representation and its underside, as de Certeau put it, is taken from Freud or Lacan rather than Marx or Hegel (1988: 48). Its formulation follows that of Freud's theory for the interpretation of dreams which is similarly built on a platform of stipulated need – the protection of sleep – that has no tangible figurative import in the ensuing hermeneutics. If we take this analogy a little further we arrive at the following rather interesting parallel: for de Certeau it is our relation to the real that is functionally equivalent to the role Freud assigns sleep. And just as wish-fulfilment is the basic means dreams have of assuring sleep, so writing as a memory-machine is history's way of providing a certain type of easement: 'As a practice (and not by virtue of the discourses that are its result) it symbolises a society capable of managing the space that it provides for itself, of replacing the obscurity of the lived body with the expression of a "will to know" or a "will to dominate" the body, of changing inherited traditions into a textual product or, in short, of being turned into a blank page that it should itself be able to write' (de Certeau, 1988: 6). The crux of de Certeau's argument is that historiography is first of all an operation which needs to be understood in terms of its function within a cultural field before it can be read for either its political or epistemological valency.

As I suggested above, his approach can be summarised as meta-historiographical because it takes the form, first of all, of an inquiry into the cultural need for historical discourse. The practice of writing history is thus contingent upon the kind of need it must satisfy and varies accordingly when this need changes. With this frame in place, we can turn now to a more specific account of de Certeau's meta-historiographic inquiry, the implication being that the historiographical operation is a kind of cultural dreamwork, easing the unconsciously felt anxiety of our culture's loss of certainty in its relation to the real following the generalised secularisation that even a religious historian like de Certeau himself admits is now all but complete. On this point it is important to bear in mind the distinction made above between writing as a machine and its products because de Certeau's argument is not that historiographic texts can be read – using the ready-made model Lacan extrapolated from Freud (which re-writes displacement as metaphor and condensation as metonym) – as straightforward outpourings of dreamwork. One has to inquire instead into the special properties of writing that enable it to ease the anxiety we all must confront, namely the fear of the unknown that is death.

History, de Certeau says, stands in the place of the real, by which he means, the place of the abysmal wound to our collective ego that is the certain knowledge that we must die. The real, on this view, resists representation absolutely, as Lacan says it does, because death itself is unpresentable. Its true face, Deleuze says (1994: 112), after Blanchot, is never seen, only our fantasised image of it gets any attention, hence our complete failure to come to grips with it, culturally speaking. How then does historiography grant us the comforting thought of immortality? This I believe is the unstated rationale behind de Certeau's inquiry into the historiographic operation which, tellingly enough, begins with a series of practical questions masquerading as ontological interrogatives: 'What do historians really fabricate when they "make history"? What are they "working on"? What do they produce? Interrupting their erudite perambulations around the rooms of the National Archives, for a moment they detach themselves from the monumental studies that will place them among their peers, and walking out into the street, they ask, "What in God's name is this business? What about the bizarre relation I am keeping with current society and, through the intermediary of my technical activities, with death?"' (de Certeau, 1988: 56). It is of course precisely those technical activities which de Certeau here mentions so off-handedly that will subsequently take up so much of his attention and to which we must now turn.

As we've seen already, de Certeau's fundamental hypothesis is that historiography must be understood as an operation. What this means, on his view, is that history can be understood as a tripartite *combinatoire* comprising of 'the relation between a *place* (a recruitment, a milieu, a profession or business, etc.), analytical *procedures* (a discipline), and the construction of a *text* (a literature). That would be to admit that it is part of the "reality" with which it deals, and that this reality can be grasped "as a human activity", or "as a practice"' (de Certeau, 1988: 57). As I mentioned in the previous chapter, the logic of this *combinatoire* (and not just the point about practices) is drawn from Marx, albeit at the price of a certain reversal of the Marxian doctrine which holds that writing is improductive labour. History writing, de Certeau argues, is usefully and legitimately treated as a form of productive labour because there can be no doubt that in our time discourse is a form of capital: 'Clearly this perspective also holds for the historian's "labour" that uses discourse as its tool; and in this respect, historiography also clearly pertains to what it must study: the relation among a *place*, a *labour*, and this "increase of capital" that can constitute *discourse*' (de Certeau, 1988: 14).

Before I expand on the make-up of this *combinatoire*, I want to underscore what I think is a rather crucial point and that is the fact that through this Marxian derived *combinatoire* de Certeau enacts a kind of negative dialectics. The aim of his many-sided analysis of historiography is, as he asserts time and again, to make history writing itself a part of what history must study. Such an ambition amounts to making history conscious of its own productions. Production, on this view, can be seen to be the means to an end, that is to say, production is de Certeau's means of a discipline-wide act of consciousness raising. The productivist hypothesis (as I will call it) is not without its risks, however; and de Certeau is extremely careful not to put it forward without a warning or two about its usage: 'So that, through "production", we will not be limited to naming a necessary but unknown relation among known terms – in other words, to designating what supports historical discourse but which is not the object of analysis – we must recall what Marx noted in his *Theses on Feuerbach*, to the effect that "the thing, reality, sensuousness" must be grasped "*as a human sensuous activity*", as a "*practice*"' (de Certeau, 1988: 13). As it turns out, the warning can also be read as an instruction in the proper use of the *combinatoire* – it makes it clear that de Certeau will not allow history to be turned into just another form of production within a generalised economy of signs.

The *combinatoire* is thus at once strategic and critical: its three points of capture, as I would rather call them, *place*, *labour* and *discourse*, furnish both a hypothesis about the nature of history writing and the means of articulating it. In what follows, then, I will try to give a sense of what the terms mean in themselves as well as a more detailed map of how they interrelate. However, so prismatic is this *combinatoire*

it is difficult to know where one might legitimately begin. Given its
later resonances in de Certeau's analyses of space and spatiality there
can be no question that of the three terms 'place' is the most important
from the perspective of the oeuvre as a whole. The significance of its
position in the present *combinatoire* is, however, much less certain
because the emphasis de Certeau places on treating history as a practice
tempts us to give priority to 'labour'. By the same token, the fact that
the productivist hypothesis itself hinges on a certain revaluation of the
notion of discourse would seem to indicate that our proper point of entry
should be there. And of course, all this gets turned around again by de
Certeau's insistence that all writing issues from a place, even his own,
so that all labour is situated and all discourse stamped with its point of
origin. In view of this, it seems clear the fulcrum of this particular
combinatoire is indeed place as we originally presumed. This view is
ratified by de Certeau's stipulation of its double function.

> The historiographic institution is inscribed within a complex that
> permits only one kind of production for it and prohibits others. Such is
> the double function of place. It makes possible certain researches
> through the fact of common conjunctures and problematics. But it
> makes others impossible; it excludes from discourse what is its basis at
> a given moment; it plays the role of a censor with respect to current –
> social, economic, political – postulates of analysis. This combination of
> permission and interdiction is doubtless the blind spot of historical
> research, and also the reason why it is incompatible with *n'importe
> quoi*, just anything. (de Certeau, 1988: 68)[4]

De Certeau's concept of 'place', as it is worked out in his critique of
historiography, anticipates by a decade or so Donna Haraway's
polemical call for 'situated knowledge' (which itself, in spite of an
absence of any such acknowledgment, doubtless recalls Sartre's still
earlier critical use of the term 'situation'): it refers to both the
institution needed to support and sponsor writing and the epistemology
underpinning it, literally the place where one writes and the place from
which one writes. I'm certain they would have agreed on the importance
of the critical practice of what Haraway calls 'positioning', which
means assuming responsibility for one's own enabling devices (concepts
fully as much as research grant monies); I'm equally certain de Certeau
would want to allow, as Haraway does, that situated knowledge requires
the 'object of knowledge be pictured as an actor and agent' (Haraway,
1991: 198). Indeed, as we've already seen, the basis of the bulk of de
Certeau's critiques of critical and sociological theory in his own time
was precisely the fact that one cannot treat knowledge as passive. Think
of his views on utopia, for instance, which turn on the fact that some of
the best of intentions have resulted in the worst of living conditions.
The signal difference between their respective positions is the obvious

fact that Haraway emphasises gender and de Certeau does not. While some (Morris, 1990; Morse, 1990) see this as a fatal flaw, I think it is more productive to see his position (taken as a whole) as enabling of exactly the kind of nuanced perspective Haraway and others subsequently produced.[5]

Place, therefore, has two mutually reinforcing senses: in the sense of the vantage point from which one writes, place is the product a deliberate temporal schism, the inaugurating split history institutes between past and present; while in the sense of the institution where one writes, place is the condition of possibility for this splitting of the historical continuum: 'First of all, historiography separates its present time from a past. But everywhere it repeats the initial act of division. Thus its chronology is composed of "periods" (for example, the Middle Ages, modern history, contemporary history) between which, in every instance, is traced the *decision* to become different or no longer to be such as one had been up to that time (the Renaissance, the French Revolution). In their respective turns, each "new" time provides the *place* for a discourse considering whatever preceded it to be "dead", but welcoming a "past" that had already been specified by former ruptures. Breakage is therefore the postulate of interpretation (which is constructed as of the present time) and its object (divisions, organising representations that must be reinterpreted)' (de Certeau, 1988: 3–4). What separates de Certeau's analysis of place from a more straightforward sort of semiotic reading is the fact that he contextualises it with an historical reading of the emergence of history itself. He asks, 'What permitted history to be born as a discipline?' His answer will enable us to situate place still more thoroughly, making it as much an example of a situated knowledge as the argument for such a thing.

The place of history, understood now as the conceptual logic enabling it to be written, did not emerge until writing itself emerged in the form in which we presently know it with the breakdown of the religious word. 'When the religious unanimity of Christendom was broken down into the diversity of European states, a knowledge was needed to take up the slack of belief and allow each group or each country to receive a distinctive definition. With the effects of the printing press, of a growing literacy and education, knowledge became a tool of unification and differentiation' (de Certeau, 1988: 26). The importance attributed to history today is a function of the fact it fulfils the role once played by religion, substituting an intricate plank of facts for the Truth. It blossomed in an ideological vacuum that needed some new strong form of an explanation to pick up where the then discredited religious form had left off. As such, it never had to question either its own history, or what amounts to the same thing, its own sources of authority and legitimacy. Belief in its stories was guaranteed by its place in society. The later panics about objectivity and narrative and such like are merely

abreactions, born of the realisation that history is more deeply grounded
in belief than it cares to think. It is this type of 'positioning' (which I
read as 'estranging') or 'historicising of history', an explicit project of
de Certeau's (1988: 21), that makes it productive to correlate de Certeau
with Brecht (1964), particularly if this amounts to reading him 'against
the grain'.

Taking place seriously is, according to de Certeau, 'the condition that
allows something to be stated that is neither legendary (or "edifying")
nor atopical (lacking relevance)' (1988: 69). To deny the specificity of
place, he adds, is the very principle of operation of ideology, whose key
instrument is the non-place. And while we can certainly agree with de
Certeau on this point, the whole of Marxist and Freudian discourse is
behind us on it (as de Certeau notes), our certainty is put into doubt by
Marc Augé's eccentric uptake of it in *Non-Places*. Whereas for de
Certeau the non-place is analogous to a form of theory-blind, false
consciousness, for Augé it is the basis of his description of a post-
postmodern, epochal shift (1995; 1998: 115–22). Non-places, by which
he simply means, contrary to de Certeau, those generic spaces we have
come to associate with modernity, such as airports, bus terminals,
underground railways, department stores, and the like, are proliferating,
he argues, and so postmodernity is slipping silently and without even a
whimper into what he calls supermodernity (an even more affect-
drained epoch than postmodernity is supposed to be on Jameson's
[1991] description of it). This version of the non-place may well be a
strong misreading of de Certeau, but I would want to add that
ultimately, and regrettably enough, it does not much deepen our
understanding of de Certeau.[6] In fact, insofar as the whole theorisation
of it in Augé's hands seems to turn on a kind nostalgia for some
mystical, pastoral type of collective existence, it could even be said to
obscure our understanding of de Certeau: for it is precisely in order to
express its collective, non-personal nature, that de Certeau ascribes it a
place.

> Akin to a car produced by a factory, the historical study is bound to the
> complex of a specific and collective fabrication more than it is the effect
> merely of a personal philosophy or the resurgence of a past 'reality'. It
> is the *product* of a *place*. (de Certeau, 1988: 64)

At this point we glide into a discussion of practices because it is the
various conventions of historical writing that guard its place, it being
understood that place is still primary because it is the condition of
possibility for the practices operating in its name. Before moving on to a
discussion of practices, it needs to be noted that place is not merely the
absent cause of the historical text, which can somehow be dismissed
because of a lack of semiotic presence. In fact, on the contrary, markers
of place – and I do not simply mean the deictics – are to be found like so

many rivets throughout the historical text holding it together at all the crucial conjunctures. I am referring, of course, to pronouns, which in different ways both Althusser (1977) and Benveniste (1971) have shown are the basic backbone of any text. While it is true de Certeau tends to favour Benveniste's explanation (along with Ducrot's important extensions), inasmuch as he recognises a certain 'hailing' function in their usage he is obviously mindful of Althusser as well. 'Without waiting for the theoretician's denunciation, the text in itself avows its relation with the institution. For example, the author's "we" refers to a convention (or, as semiotics would cast the formula, it refers to an "enunciative verisimilitude"). In the text, the "we" stages a social contract "among ourselves", in which the plural subject "utters" the discourse. A "we" takes hold of language for itself by virtue of being placed in the speaking subject's position' (de Certeau, 1988: 63; see also Carrard 1992: 93–5). The convention of using the plural form, the global 'we', ensures, in the manner of the father's name, the pre-eminence of History over all histories.

By the same token, it has a community function as well: 'The authorial "we" corresponds to that of true readers' (de Certeau, 1988: 68). History is not truly read by the general public, even if it is their patronage which ultimately, that is, in the final instance, supports the production of history through their subscription to journals, their consumption of popular historical works and their taxes. Rather, history is read by historians, who reserve the right of judgement and from whom one receives proper accreditation as a historian. What this amounts to saying, though, is that history is in itself a practice: it is something that certain people, with the appropriate qualifications and training, do, in the course of their working lives. It is thus a kind of discourse that, historically and sociologically speaking, is inaugurated by a set of relations between people. History as concept and discourse was born, not all at once, but in fits, of the foundation of several interrelated professional bodies and special interest groups in the seventeenth-century, at a time when universities were in a state of decline having become overly isolationist (de Certeau, 1988: 61). Its early mentors were the insatiably curious travellers of the period, some of whom are today recognised as the forerunners to anthropology as well (Montaigne, Lafitau and Léry, for instance). History was their means of 'staging' their curious discoveries: it was thus, in the first instance, and still, a community-based language experiment. The first job of history writing was to find a form – narrative – capable of accommodating both the discoveries themselves and the sense of wonder they originally aroused in the discoverers themselves (de Certeau 1988: 60). Here, then, anticipating Bourdieu by several years, is an outline for an analysis of the discipline of history as a form of 'cultural production'.

Never what you could call a card-carrying Marxist, de Certeau became interested in practices not out of some hitherto undisclosed radical sensibility, but because he wanted to find the means of transforming the readily observable, although not then theorised, correlation between historians as a social group and their productions, namely books of history, into a causal relation. Even so, he did uphold the basic Marxist principle that the only acceptable theory is one that takes account of practice. His premise was that the 'same movement organises society and the "ideas" that circulate within it' (de Certeau, 1988: 61). What de Certeau realised, which was to prove transformative of his view of things, is that history's practices are inseparable from its methods, that in effect, these are one and the same. His principle evidence for this argument is the fact that, as he demonstrates, methods are themselves entirely contingent upon the establishment of place, which is to say, they only become possible and only finally make sense within the special confines of one (de Certeau, 1988: 58). Methods, he argued, 'define the parameters of institutional behaviour and the laws of a milieu' (de Certeau, 1988: 65). Or, to put it another way, if practices and methods were somehow primordially distinct from one another, such a differentiation would have to be at the price of treating method as an autonomous discourse, which to de Certeau's way of thinking is the supreme duplicity because it permits the denial of place (1988: 65).

Situating history as a practice among others in a larger milieu enables de Certeau to show that it is itself subject to the seed-born influences of the times. 'Is it by chance that we move from "social history" to "economic history" between the two wars, around the time of the Great Depression of 1929; or that cultural history wins out at the moment when the social, economic, and political importance of 'culture' is felt everywhere through mass media and leisure time?' (de Certeau, 1988: 66). Of course one could continue this list indefinitely, but a litany of coincidences does not amount to proof, however compelling such concatenations might be. Rather what we need to see is evidence that the atmosphere of the times is in some way built into the very mechanism of historical discourse. De Certeau shows that indirectly, but no less concretely for being so, the climate of the times influences history by acting like a censor or filter, determining what can and cannot count as history on the basis of some never properly articulated criteria of current aptness. History's own reality principle is the collective biases of its true readers: only in secular times, for instance, is it possible to write a *history* of religion; without that feeling of separation, one is destined to remain *inside* and thus blind to one's own fatalities, but even more crucially, without that separation one would not be permitted to comment on one's own fatalities. As de Certeau puts it, striking a distinctly Lukácsian note, 'social changes provides historical distance in relation to what is becoming an entirely past time' (1988: 67).

All of this can be brought into sharper relief, I will suggest, by comparing de Certeau's (meta-)theorisation of historiography to Jameson's notion of metacommentary, which similarly uses a Freudian model, but gives history a very different part to play. Metacommentary, which is designed to account for (and indeed insist upon the need to question) our felt need for interpretation, 'implies a model not unlike the Freudian hermeneutic (divested, to be sure, of its own specific content, of the topology of the unconscious, the nature of the libido, and so forth), one based on the distinction between symptom and repressed idea, between manifest and latent content, between the disguise and the message disguised' (Jameson, 1988a: 13). In other words, it amounts to supposing from the outset, as with more traditional kinds of hermeneutics, that all texts are somehow at the mercy of a censor, that whatever is manifest in them is in fact a necessary distortion of a true, but forcefully rendered latent content. 'Thus, the process of criticism is not so much an interpretation of content as it is a revealing of it, a laying bare, a restoration of the original message, the original experience, from beneath the distortions of the censor: and this revelation takes the form of an explanation why the content was so distorted; it is inseparable from a description of the mechanism of censorship itself' (Jameson, 1988a: 14). Crucially, as he notes in later works, Jameson (1981: 65; 1992a: 25) recognises that insofar as one does follow Freud's model everything has to be read under the sign of wish-fulfilment, this being the instrumental postulate of all Freud's interpretative strategies.

On this view, the content presents itself to us as the gratifying answer to a question we cannot remember asking, but whose urgency we somehow feel anyway. What the critic has to figure out, then, is why the original content needed to be distorted in the first place, why, in other words, couldn't it have been presented in some less mediated form, and, moreover, why it should have been distorted in this particular way. In the analysis of dreams, the distortion evident in the manifest content is explained in terms of a need to protect sleep from the residual anxieties of the day's events, which cannot simply be gotten rid of, but must somehow be accommodated, literally, as one accommodates unruly house guests – who cannot just be evicted (because they are family, or whatever) – by placating them. Our mind's recourse, via the dreamwork, is to transform the lingering images of the day's petty and not so petty traumas and other angst inducing episodes into little stories with happy endings. Dreams make true what in the course of the day we could only wish. What the dreamwork seems to recognise is that we cannot be content, that is, cannot sleep, unless we have closure; but, and this is crucial, it doesn't matter to us very much whether that closure is real or symbolic, either will do just so long as we get it. As such, the dream is genuinely a symbolic satisfaction of a real need. In waking life, so the Marxian uptake of psychoanalysis has argued, we have a similar need of pacification which is similarly answered by symbolic means, which, bluntly speaking, accounts for the social significance of those items we customarily refer to as 'cultural' – film, literature, theatre, and even historiography.

This is Jameson's way of arguing against merely repressive or too straightforwardly coercive theories of ideology: we could not be persuaded by an ideology, he argues, if it did not, however minimally, fulfil something we had already, perhaps even under different circumstances, wished for (1992a: 25). Manipulation, he argues, must always pay the price of offering a utopian possibility of radical change, even when it issues from an utterly conservative institution, such as that of the capitalist mode of production itself. Pure, violent repression is never so powerfully tranquillising as a sugar-coated pill we swallow not merely voluntarily or willingly, but have actively fought for the right to take. For Jameson, the manufacturer of this savage little pill, as we might call it with apologies to Alanis Morissette, is of course late capitalism; what this means, though, is that the censor in our time is late capitalism, as a present and ongoing social system, not history as a recording process, as it is for de Certeau. Rather for Jameson history is, as he puts it, that untranscendable horizon which, inasmuch as it corresponds to the experience of Necessity itself, by which he means the inexorable form of events rather than a particular sort of content, 'needs no particular theoretical justification'. We may be sure, he judiciously adds, 'that its alienating necessities will not forget us, however much we might prefer to ignore them' (Jameson, 1981: 102). Narrative, as Hayden White explains, is the means Jameson proposes for coming to grips with necessity (1987: 149).

On this point, de Certeau and Jameson are in agreement – but for de Certeau history is nothing but narrative, whereas for Jameson narrative is only one of many ways of accessing it. Indeed, against the current of times, the fashion of referring to everything as textual mentioned above, Jameson insisted that history is precisely *not* a text, even if it can only be accessed as such (1981: 35). De Certeau, as should now be obvious, could never countenance this transcendental use of history because it grants it exactly the kind of autonomy he is at pains to dismantle (I hesitate to say deconstruct, though it may well be applicable). If one were to read Jameson from de Certeau's point of view, one would have to ask just what his notion of history refers to, how it is constructed, and whence it is derived? In other words, it is all very well to 'always historicise' but one must always historicise history too! Such an analysis is famously repudiated in advance by Jameson, but if one swaps a sociological perspective for a philosophical one, such a repudiation begins to look more like a mechanism of defence than an irrefrangible 'coup'. De Certeau would emphasise that Jameson's use of history is precisely practical, not philosophical, or if it is, then philosophy is already a kind of consciousness of community. What de Certeau's meta-theorisation of historiography does, then, is destroy the false god of History. We can guess why. In so doing, he creates a yawning gap – a gap which doubles, as it were, the initial gap history was itself supposed to paper over. Under the auspices of heterology, de Certeau performs a kind of metacommentary on history as a concept. Having exposed the all too human side of history as a practice, he then tackles its metaphysical pretensions.

Notes

[1] Using a similarly constructed argument, Haraway argues that science is the myth of today (1991: 42; 81).

[2] 'If one wishes to connect a mythical schema to a general history, to explain how it corresponds to the interests of a definite society – in short, to pass from semiology to ideology, it is obviously at the level of the third type of focusing that one must place oneself: it is the reader of myths himself who must reveal their essential function' (Barthes, 1972: 139).

[3] As Ricoeur shows, for psychoanalysis, dreams are paradoxical because they imply the unity of two contradictory orders: fulfilment and repression (1970: 92).

[4] It is worth noting that Jameson (1981) also ascribes the role of censor to history, in his schematisation of the political unconscious.

[5] For an evaluation of de Certeau's usefulness to feminism along precisely these critical, but pragmatic lines, see Langbauer, 1999, and Scott, 1991: 51.

[6] For my reading of Augé, see Buchanan, 1999.

4. Heterology, or the book we'll never read[1]

> When one says that heterology scientifically considers questions of
> heterogeneity, one does not mean that heterology is, in the usual sense
> of such a formula, the science of the heterogeneous.
>
> Georges Bataille, *Visions of Excess*

As he was writing what would turn out to be his last books, the two
volumes on seventeenth-century French mysticism, de Certeau was
already sketching a future project which was to have been an analysis of
what he referred to as heterological thinking in early anthropological
discourse. The title of the collection of his essays translated into English
just prior to his untimely death, *Heterologies: Discourse on the Other*,
anticipates this never to be completed book and clearly signals that
work on it had already commenced. Indeed, according to his literary
executor, Luce Giard, three chapters of this book – 'we will never read'
(1991a: 213) – can already be found in de Certeau's existing work: one
is in *Heterologies* (on Montaigne), another is in *The Writing of History*
(on Léry), and a third (on Lafitau), yet to be anthologised, is published
in an issue of *Yale Journal of French Studies* devoted to the origins of
anthropological writing.[2] Each of these essays is concerned with the
way these forerunners to modern anthropology – Montaigne, Léry and
Lafitau – encountered the manifold differences of the New World as
alterity and turned that alterity into a means of authorising their own
discourse about the Old World.

The intellectual basis of this project can already been seen, as I
suggested in the previous chapter, in de Certeau's critique of
historiography. In fact, I would go so far as to say that work raised the
very questions heterology was intended to investigate further and
hopefully answer. By defining history as a confrontation with alterity in
the psychoanalytic way he did, de Certeau furnishes himself with the
means of answering the question he posed of why we should need
history. However, in doing so he knowingly raises – but never
effectively answers – a host of more directly philosophical questions
which are not easily recuperated by the same means. A metaphysical

inquiry into our relation with death is thus built into the psychological inquiry. These two strands coalesce to form a new kind of hermeneutic demand or program which de Certeau proposed to call 'heterology'.[3] Richard Terdiman summarises its project as follows: 'Heterology seeks to grant full credit to the *otherness* of alterity – to its capacity *not* simply to be a mystified effect of the observer's own system and discourse. The problem, both for our theory and for our practice, is to see how to imagine a communication circuit between authentically different entities, a circuit truly bilateral' (1992: 7). To which I want to add, the very conditions of the problem incapacitate in advance any solution except a kind of Deleuzian transcendental empiricist one.

In the undecided swerving between the Lacanian Other and the Leviansian Other, we have the philosophical problematic which forms the basis of de Certeau's great unfinished project 'heterology'. (De Certeau seems not to have been inspired by Bataille, though it is possible he took the term 'heterology' from him and creatively misread it because for Bataille it similarly refers to a manipulation of the possibilities of the sacred [Bataille, 1985: 96]. However, there is no evidence to support this surmise save the interesting coincidence of terminology.) Begun while still in the USA, the heterological project was put on hold so he could complete his work on mysticism, and – regrettably – never resumed. Since de Certeau died before formulating either a specific thesis or a particular method, we have no certain way of knowing what he actually intended by the term. Even so, by taking the path of the 'negative' (that which the dialectic purposively excludes) as de Certeau sometimes called it, it may be possible to construct a workable impression of what heterology is by determining what it decidedly is not. While it is true that we do not really know what 'heterology' is meant to stand for, it is quite clear from his existing work that he wanted to steer cultural studies (at least the incipient form of it that existed prior to his death in 1986) away from the 'phenomenological' mode of hermeneutics popularised by Clifford Geertz, among others.

To put it simply, de Certeau rejected 'phenomenological hermeneutics' because at bottom it presumes that the state of affairs called culture is, through being composed of 'expressive symbols', a purely relative, or at best *quid pro quo*, structure. Geertz's 'interpretative anthropology' is exemplary in this respect. He avers that like lives, societies 'contain their own interpretations', leaving theory the task of learning 'how to gain access to them' (Geertz, 1973: 453). 'What is needed', he therefore argues, 'is some systematic, rather than merely literary or impressionistic' (Geertz, 1973: 364) way of discovering and ultimately articulating the given *as the given*. This would involve laying bare the 'conceptual structure embodied in the symbolic forms through which persons are perceived actually is'

(Geertz, 1973: 364). According to Geertz, what cultural studies requires methodologically, but does not yet have, is 'a developed method of describing and analysing the meaningful structure of experience' as it is 'apprehended by representative members of a particular society at a particular point in time' (Geertz, 1973: 364). What is wanted, therefore, is 'a scientific phenomenology of culture' (Geertz, 1973: 364). Such an enterprise, as Geertz later described it (1983: 5), is an attempt to understand understanding, and insofar as hermeneutics is understood to mean just that he is happy to accept that label for his work.

The culture as puzzle view ('The trick is to figure out what the devil they think they are up to' [Geertz, 1983: 58]) advocated by Geertz is predicated on an unbridgeable divide – absolute heterogeneity – between the ethnographer and his or her subject, or what in philosophical terms amounts to the division between the Same and the Other. What Geertz endeavours to articulate are particularised worldviews, or perspectives. As he points out, no doubt correctly, the ethnographer is not able to perceive what his or her informants perceive. All that the ethnographer can hope to grasp – 'and that uncertainly enough' (Geertz, 1983: 58) – is the apparatus which, at a deep conceptual level, the 'informants' 'perceive "with" – or "by means of", or "through" ... or whatever the word should be' (Geertz, 1983: 58). Then, the ethnographer can produce something like a map – a diagrammatization – of the vital concepts through which everyday life is lived. However, the vitality of these concepts does not survive their articulation, and whatever it is that ethnography does articulate it is not, as we saw in a previous chapter, the *vital* concepts through which everyday life is lived. These remain beyond grasp, apparently infinitely other. This is a paradigmatic example of what may be usefully circumscribed as the problem of otherness. Although Geertz acknowledges the depth and significance of this problem, he never seriously engages with it himself. In fact, perhaps betraying a weariness with postmodernist debate, he places it beyond the grasp of anyone to solve.

> If the relation of what we write to what we write about, Morocco, say, or Indonesia, can no longer be credibly compared with that of a map to a distant territory or to that of a sketch to an exotic animal recently come upon, what can it be compared with? Telling a believable story? Building a workable model? Translating an alien language? Construing an enigmatical text? Conducting an intelligible dialogue? Excavating a buried site? Staging an instructive illustration? (Geertz, 1995: 98)

All these possibilities, he adds, have been suggested. But none, he implies, have greater credibility, or more importantly, greater intellectual cogency, than the analogy of a map to a distant territory. The problem with this cognitive model is, as de Certeau has pointed out, that it turns time into space (1984: 97). Unlike the defeatist Geertz, de Certeau does in fact perceive there to be another way, a means other than analogy: heterology. What is admirable in de Certeau's critique of the position adopted by Geertz is the fact that while remaining critical he does not simply succumb to the manifold seductions of nihilism and push aside a too optimistic positivism in favour of a gloatingly negative relativism. De Certeau's position thus needs to be distinguished from Geertz's successors, some of whom, like the ones Geertz scathingly calls Malinowski's children (1988: 73–101), do seem to have fallen for the blandishments of a Rorty type pragmatic relativism. De Certeau does not allow that it is enough merely to posit that cultural studies *is* writing, and that writing *is* intrinsically metaphorical and therefore able to deliver only partial truths, which is all James Clifford (Malinowskian son, par excellence, in the Bloomian/oedipal sense) does, but searches for a more adequate mode of expression. Heterology would have been this 'more adequate mode of expression'.

To get some idea of the necessity of constructing a 'more adequate mode of expression' one has only to witness the nihilism of Clifford's work. Echoing Hayden White's (1973; 1978) earlier shattering of that certainty of historiography so cherished by historians, namely objective writing (Novick, 1988: 1), Clifford is content to recite the postmodern axiom that truth is always already partial, at best, because it is written. Ethnographers, as writers, 'cannot avoid expressive tropes, figures, and allegories that select and impose meaning as they translate it' (Clifford, 1986a: 7). The implication of this view, which Clifford suggests is 'more Nietzschean than realist or hermeneutic', is that 'all constructed truths are made possible by powerful "lies" of exclusion and rhetoric' (Clifford, 1986a: 7). Cultural studies must recognise, therefore, that even the 'best ethnographic texts', or what he calls 'serious, true fictions', have to be rethought in terms of 'systems, or economies, of truth' (Clifford, 1986a: 7). Power is implicit in these systems, and it works through them 'in ways their authors cannot fully control' (Clifford, 1986a: 7). However, the problem, as Derrida shows, is more complex than this, and not only epistemological in nature: 'There is no ethics without the presence *of the other* but also, and consequently, without absence, dissimulation, detour, differance, writing' (1974:139–40).

In other words, allegorisation, which erodes the other by privileging the 'detour' of writing, is incapable of being ethical. It is just this conclusion that de Certeau will not allow. The difficulty is that the problem which de Certeau must address to restore ethics is practically insoluble. For while the presence of the other is the condition of possibility for ethics, its absence is the condition of possibility for otherness. So, unless cultural studies can reconcile the logically irreconcilable, a just ethnography remains beyond its grasp. In

philosophy where there is already an established tradition of debate
concerning the relation between Same and Other, namely heterology, a
similar problem exists. The problem is articulated in two different ways:
on the one hand, there is the fear that the Other, if it is prediscursive,
which is to say always already constituted, will 'crush' the Same; and
on the other hand, the fear is that the Same, if it is constitutive, such as
is the case in phenomenology, will absorb the Other. As Merleau-Ponty
puts it, 'Insofar as I constitute the world, I cannot conceive another
consciousness, for it too would have to constitute the world and, at least
as regards this other view of the world, I should not be the constituting
agent' (1962: 350).

Traditionally, 'heterology' designates that branch of philosophy
concerned with the other as that which philosophy relies on without
being able to comprehend. Corresponding to the first 'problem', the
Other in this case, besides being 'what I am not', 'where I am not', and
'when I am not', is also infinite and radically contiguous – which is to
say, so beyond imagining that it does not even share a common border
with the imaginable. God, obviously, meets all of these requirements but
that does not mean the Other *must be* construed theologically. In fact,
an unconscious deification (the structural equivalent of the projection of
phantasms in a psychoanalytic sense) is one of the risks of heterology.
Montaigne's 'Of Cannibals', for instance, is, according to de Certeau,
'inscribed within this heterological tradition, in which the discourse
about the other is a means of constructing a discourse authorised by the
other'.[4] As an absolute Other the Cannibal is Godlike in his ability to
guarantee the Word.

As Levinas shows, when a theological Other conditions thought, it
reduces the subject to a state of passivity. Our relationship with the
Other is always, he says, a relationship with Mystery (1987: 75).
Mystery, of which death is obviously enough the supreme example, is
that which incapacitates us, that which deprives us of the ability to act
by overwhelming our senses. Contrary to Heidegger who asserts that the
thought of death empowers *Dasein* – which we take to mean 'us' – with
its fullest 'potentiality-for-Being' (Heidegger, 1962: 294), Levinas
argues that such thoughts of death, by bringing the subject to the limit
of the possible, leave him or her no 'longer able to be able' (1987: 74).
What the subject is no longer able to do, in the face of death, is *grasp
the initiative*. So complete is the strangeness of the future of death that
it renders the subject utterly immobile (Levinas, 1987: 81). And,
Levinas says, it 'is exactly thus that the subject loses its very mastery as
a subject' (1987: 74). The other is the all-powerful before whom 'we'
passively stand in judgement.

For Lyotard, this 'passivity' constitutes the very value and advantage
of Levinas's thought. What it expresses is the fact that insofar as I am
spoken to 'the place of the one who speaks to me is never available to

me to occupy' (Lyotard and Thébaud, 1985: 39). That is to say, it is always the other who speaks, not me. In many respects, the central problem of the *differend* (the impossibility of finding an adequate phrase to articulate wrongs [Lyotard, 1988: 5], and, concomitantly, the impossibility of determining adequate criteria for justice [Lyotard and Thébaud, 1985: 14–15]) is a Levinasian one.[5] It reiterates precisely Levinas's primary problem: 'How can a being enter into a relation with the other without allowing its very self to be crushed by the other?' (1987: 77) In other words, how can a victim become a plaintiff? How can a victim of a wrong, remembering that by definition a victim is bereft of the means of proving the occurrence of a wrong, give testimony against an other when to do so means speaking in the other's place? (Lyotard, 1988: 9). Insofar as the speech situation is that of a tribunal it is the law that speaks, not the victim, and it is this place that he or she must occupy to become a plaintiff.

But in doing so they lose control of their testimony. How, Levinas asks, can one avoid being crushed by this other? Like Levinas, Lyotard locates this problem in discourse, or more specifically in the pragmatics of the speech encounter; unlike Levinas however, whose model is the conversation,[6] Lyotard's is the tribunal, which allows him to depict the political as an agonistics between Self and Other.[7] The other for Lyotard is an oppressive weight of prescription that cannot be attenuated because its axioms precede and therefore condition the situation wherein redress is sought. Justice, in this case, is only possible insofar as one is able to free oneself from the obligations imposed by the other (Lyotard and Thébaud, 1985: 41–2). Perhaps defining the difference between the coeval, but basically heterogeneous enterprises of postmodernism and deconstruction, Lyotard's definition of justice is the reverse of Derrida's (1994: 36), wherein the other must be freed from the obligations of the Same before justice can prevail.[8] Even so, it is noteworthy that in both cases justice is a matter for a still to be specified futurology. In both cases, the just is that (in the Same) which sustains an open future, one free from obligations. The Same, for both Lyotard (1988: 105) and Derrida (1994: 34), philosophically transcribes the social as a relatively homogeneous, or at least hegemonically stable, bloc or assemblage. It is not determined by an extant state of affairs, however, but rather by an internal logic of conformity, a will not to be different.

Why Derrida and Lyotard differ can be appreciated in terms of the way their respective definitions of the other varies. Both, of course, maintain that the other is 'what I am not', 'where I am not', and 'when I am not', but Derrida in contrast to Lyotard, refuses the traditional heterological definition of the absolutely other.[9] In fact, Derrida relegates heterology to the lowly rank of hollow dream (1978: 151). Yet in doing so he opens the way for a critical heterology such as the one de

Certeau hoped to formulate. Derrida's critique of a specific concept or notion creates a rupture through which heterology emerges as a new mode of analysis. In a long essay on Levinas, Derrida argues that a '*purely* heterological' (1978: 151) structure of thought, which is to say a structure of thought that radically distinguishes Same and Other, is the naive dream of empiricism. According to Derrida, by 'radicalizing the theme of the infinite exteriority of the other' Levinas assumes an identical aim (albeit with greater audacity) to the one which 'has more or less secretly animated all the philosophical gestures which have been called *empiricisms* in the history of philosophy' (1978: 151). In other words, by 'making the origin of language, meaning, and difference the relation to the infinitely other' (Derrida, 1978: 151) Levinas is compelled to relinquish conceptuality, which is to say philosophy.[10] His philosophy which is, perhaps in spite of itself, a philosophy of immanence, cannot sustain the concept as a transcendental a priori without admitting that coherence *in* incoherence – that is to say, the incoherence of the relation between the Same and the infinitely Other, which, because it insists on a radical disjuncture, is no relation at all – is possible. Without the possibility of forging coherence *in* incoherence philosophy is constrained to contemplation which, Deleuze and Guattari argue, is *not* the function of philosophy (1994: 6). Yet that is all Levinas's muted philosopher can manage – he or she stands before the Other as the plaintiff stands before the tribunal, a beggar whose fate is not their own.

So for Derrida 'heterology' is a pejorative. It stands for a philosophy that in consequence of an assiduous adherence to an absolutely binomial structure of thought, which is to say a philosophy conditioned by the disjunctive, is in fact a non-philosophy. Of course, in Bataille's hands, heterology stands for the opposite of philosophy whereby philosophy refers to 'the deprivation of our universe's sources of excitation and the development of a servile human species' (1985: 97). It isn't certain if this is precisely the sense in which de Certeau takes up the term, but it seems clear that he was interested in positing some kind of systemic alterity which would certainly be consonant with Bataille's usage. As de Certeau reveals in the work of Freud (as well as in that of Bourdieu and Durkheim), the supposition of an absolute other is an intellectual ruse by which means the rigour of philosophy is evaded. Such would be the final form, as we speculated in the previous chapter, of de Certeau's critique of Jameson's use of history. In Freud, it is the so-called ordinary man that fulfils this function. Posited as 'the representative of an abstract universal', the ordinary man plays, in Freudian theory, 'the role of a god who is recognizable in his effects' (de Certeau, 1984: 3), albeit a humbled god submerged in the superstitions of common people. The ordinary man provides Freud's discourse with the means of '*generalizing* a particular knowledge and of *guaranteeing* its validity by the whole of history' (de Certeau, 1984: 3). Although the initial sense in which de Certeau used the term 'heterology' was critical, or purely classificatory, I would argue that de Certeau intended, additionally, for it to broach a *constructivist* approach to cultural analysis, and this is the project he left unfinished.

If we define cultural studies as the concerted effort to *articulate* culture, that is to say, to *write it*, then a number of problems become immediately apparent. The principal of these, one which eclipses all the others, is the problem of *writing* itself. But this problem is too general: it must be refined before we can even begin to confront it. To engage with this problem cultural studies needs to take its reflexivity much further than it presently does. Important meta-critiques of anthropological – ethnographic – *mis-en-scene*, such as those instigated by Talal Asad (1973), and after him Edward Said (1993) (who expands the scope of the scene to include the writing of literature), and James Clifford (1986b) (whose war cry is that all ethnographic writing is allegorical), only engage with the issue of 'What *is* said?', leaving aside the more important question of 'What *can* be said?'. This 'problem' has both an epistemological and ethical dimension; it is, *at once*, an orthopractic question: can a just ethnography be written?; *and* a complex philosophical problem: can the other speak *as* other? By just, or better justice, I mean, as Derrida puts it, the 'affirmative experience of the coming of the other as other' (1994: 36). Thus, a just ethnography – heterology – is one that permits the other to speak *as* other.[11]

So what would 'heterology' look like? All that can be said, on the basis of the foregoing, is what it must be like, and that is what I will confine myself to stating. It would have to be formulated as an alternative to, but not as a compromise between, the two impossible positions outlined above: the impossibility of the infinitely other; and the impossibility of an other that is not infinitely other.[12] If cultural studies is permitted to construct its object as infinitely other, then it unavoidably construes it as mysterious, which prevents it from ever being able to articulate its position, and, more worryingly, licenses its lack of concern. If it is impossible to speak for the other, then why try? The alternative is equally problematic: if the other is not infinitely other then cultural studies would be entitled to, and quite capable of, speaking on its behalf. This risks the subsumption of the other. As we have seen, there is no compromise to be had between these two positions, so a solution, such that one is possible, must be sought elsewhere. This is why I have suggested de Certeau meant to develop a constructivist mode of cultural studies – it is the only way, or at least the only way I have encountered, out of this impasse.

Instead of positing the existence of the Same and Other, what I am calling constructivism – which I take from Deleuze and Guattari (1994)

– would argue that each is still becoming, and therefore never yet infinitely other, so it is always possible to articulate at least some aspect of its discourse. By the same token, insofar as it is becoming-infinitely-other, some part always remains outside the grasp of that attempt at articulation, so it can never be subsumed. Heterology, then, models itself not on the tribunal or the conversation, though it participates in both, but on a kind of empiricist philosophy that Deleuze (1994) called transcendental empiricism. Transcendental empiricism is the name Deleuze gave to his version of pluralism. De Certeau used no such fancy name as this, but he was nonetheless a pluralist of the same ilk. In his meditations on the city and the difficulties it poses to analysis, de Certeau formulated a precisely transcendental empiricist conclusion. Neither the bird's-eye view (the symbolic equivalent of the transcendental), nor the curb-side view (the symbolic equivalent of the empirical or immanent), he found, can provide a completely satisfactory articulation of the city since both of necessity exclude the other (de Certeau, 1984: 91–5). What de Certeau did then was to suggest a way in which both views could be simultaneously expressed: it is this way that the logic of practice announces itself as necessary and more importantly as implicitly heterological.

Indeed, I want to suggest that a programme essay for the never written book on heterology, which (albeit speculatively) enables us to read as coherent what otherwise appears disparate, can be found in *The Practice of Everyday Life*. Obviously intended as a preliminary sketch for a later work – as much of that book really is, hence its incredible suggestiveness no doubt – the chapter entitled, 'The Quotation of Voices', describes a programme of study comparable to what one finds in the strictly heterological pieces, but broader in scope. It argues that there are two distinct 'practices of the different', both of which have already been mentioned. Taken as the basis for a programme of study, as I believe it in reality is, the first category, which de Certeau calls 'the science of fables' corresponds to the essays on Montaigne, Léry and Lafitau, while the second, which he calls 'returns and turns of voice', refers to the commentaries on Durkheim, Freud, Bourdieu and Foucault (de Certeau, 1984: 156). This suggests not only that de Certeau envisaged his inquiry having at least two strands, but also that heterology is but one response to a more general problem. Now, assuming he was able to overcome his evident distaste for synoptically organised books, I imagine the heterological book would have brought these two strands together more fully than the present attempts do because as the programme essay makes clear, they are two modes of the same practice, namely, making the other speak through quotation.

What this essay ostensibly broaches is an inquiry into the disappearance of orality in the modern world, but as I aim to show, its central insights in fact underpin much of de Certeau's more general and theoretical claims, both as an analogon or model and as historical precedent. Before I flesh out this extrapolation, however, let me first provide the detail needed to make de Certeau's problem statement cogent. 'The Quotation of Voices' begins with the signal observation that an epistemological crisis arose as the view that all language and consequently all meaning originated with God was steadily eroded by sixteenth-century scholarship which by exposing the agency of authors in transforming and disseminating God's word eventually revoked the foundational resemblance between words and things (de Certeau, 1984: 137; Foucault, 1970: 40). The rise of print and the corresponding proliferation of texts resulted in the asking of a question never before contemplated: who *wrote* the text? When the author of a sacred text is known to be God, then one can take the text at its word; it has only to be read and understood, not made. If the certainty of authorial-identity this non-reflexive mode of reading relies on is destroyed, then so too is the value of the word it expresses. Now, in place of the devoted attention to statements characteristic of medieval monks, one had (in the manner of a detective?[13]) to focus on the act of producing them, on the enunciation rather than the énoncé, with the aim of determining a substitute figure for the lost ubiquity (de Certeau, 1984: 138). Accordingly, the defining question of the Classical Age was: 'who speaks when there is no longer a divine Speaker who founds every particular enunciation?' (de Certeau, 1984: 156).

In order to understand the answer which eventually emerged to this key question, one has to first of all appreciate the nature of the crisis. If the word of God is the undisputed source of all order and authority in the social world, then logically its loss of credibility will be chaos and disorder (which may be felt as either anomie or freedom). In the absence of an unchallengeable authority, the decisive parameters of everyday life lose their sharp edges, their very ability to define a person's place in other words, and suddenly a vacuum appears where previously a profound plenitude had reigned. According to de Certeau, this is precisely what happened: Where once a mysterious and divine Other had served as the basis of all meaning, now there was only others – that is, man, a poor babbling substitute for the Supreme Being. What might have been felt as freedom, as a liberation from received meanings, was rather felt as loss. Fortunately, the very instrument of the dissolution of the sacred text, writing, also provided the means of its replacement. Since writing is creation, and creation the province of God, writers occupy His place, or so it came to be thought by seventeenth-century scholars.[14] And so the subject was born. The answer that was finally settled upon (which in the eighteenth-century served as the central moral and ethical pillar of the Enlightenment) was: it is the individual subject who speaks.

> In other words, it is because he [sic] loses his position that the individual comes into being as a *subject*. The place a cosmological language formerly assigned to him and which was understood as a 'vocation' and a placement in the order of the world, becomes a 'nothing', a sort of void, which drives the subject to make himself master of a space and to set himself up as a producer of writing. (de Certeau, 1984: 138)

This shift from an oral to a scriptural economy (as de Certeau paints it), marks for de Certeau the birth of the modern, the instauration of a new episteme and a new regime of the body and law whose axioms continue to determine our existence today (1984: 144). Henceforward it was not God, but the Subject, who spoke, and it was human law, not His law, that constituted the essential limits and potential of everyday life in the Classical Age. Writing becomes power in this tumultuous era because it is capable of achieving its assigned task of producing order, of inscribing order on 'the body of an uncivilised or depraved society' (de Certeau, 1984: 144). Hence the intimacy between writing, history and death. As such, writing was the primary engine of the Reformation, which operated on the principle, or myth, that Scripture can provide, 'in the midst of a corrupt society and a decadent Church, a model one can use to re-form both society and the Church' (de Certeau, 1984: 144). It obtained as a new model of order because it was economical and discrete (or at least able to appear delimited just as the word of God once had), the margins of the page serving as its most powerful symbol of efficiency, whereas speech was nuanced and fugacious. And, we should recall, it is precisely as a form of social technology that de Certeau endeavours to apprehend writing in *The Writing of History*, which, in consequence, may just as well have been named the 'History of Writing'. In de Certeau's view, the shift from an oral to scriptural economy is *the necessary forerunner* to the reign of panopticism Foucault presents as the ubiquitous power-technology of this period because before Bentham's system of light could be put into effect, writing already presented transparency as an ideal and itself as the model and inspiration for this type of regime (1984: 145).

So, as *Robinson Crusoe* evokes rather well, writing is not simply one means of communicating among many others, but an instrumental component of everyday life. Indeed, as the castaway narrative of *Robinson Crusoe* makes especially explicit, writing is the condition of possibility for the individualist life it implicitly endorses. Crusoe takes control of his island and by implication his life by composing a diary in which he does not merely recount life on the island, but constructs the island as text: he surveys it by walking everywhere on it, he maps it by distributing place-names, and he counts its contents, then carefully records it all in his ledger. And just when his sovereignty seems perfect, when all alterity has been expunged by his diligent textualising, his world is put in disarray by the appearance of a footprint, a smudge on his pristine margin as it were. Likewise, de Certeau suggests, speech did not disappear altogether from the field of social and political discourse, but returned through cracks and fissures the scriptural space either deliberately made available, through quotation for instance, or could not ever fully control, such as the disturbing rantings of the mad and the possessed which neither quotation nor obstinate ignorance can ever adequately contain. Both of these forms of return, what we might call the controlled and uncontrolled, are to be found in *Robinson Crusoe*.

To begin with, obviously enough, in spite of his apparently well-founded, not to mention arrogant, self-assurance that he is the undisputed master of all that he surveys, a footprint still appears on *his* beach, and Crusoe can do nothing in response but bolster his already considerable defences. Henceforward, as though the footprint had somehow been impressed on his mind, where it weighs like the proverbial nightmare, he cannot think of anything else but the threat this discovery might pose (Defoe, 1985: 162). Interestingly, in reckoning his options in view of the discovery that his island is subject to visitation by what he fears are cannibals, Crusoe elects not to make pre-emptive strikes (as we would call them today) upon the savages because his conscience tells him that justice demands they be treated as innocent until proven guilty. He reaffirms this decision by declaring that as savages they are alien to him and accordingly their affairs none of his business. So in the name of the savage as citizen, the respect for which he finds sadly wanting in the Conquistadores, he decides not to exterminate them unless they attack him first (Defoe, 1985: 178). In the first instance, then, the footprint, as the mark of the other, is an extra-text, or supplement, that disproves the integrity of the text on which it appears. In the latter instance, the voice of the other serves as a pre-text for commentary, its otherness makes the production of that text possible (de Certeau, 1984: 156). De Certeau suggests that an outline of just these two 'variants', that is, the voice of the other as (1) pre-text or (2) extra-text, can serve as both a 'preliminary to the examination of oral practices' and a means of dramatising the fact the framework of the scriptural economy 'still leaves voices ways of speaking' (1984: 156).

It is the persistence of these voices in a regime that would otherwise eradicate them that is de Certeau's principal interest. And it is his attempt to schematise the methods by which such voices are able to persist that serves as the basis of his more general articulation of what may be termed cultural logic, namely strategy and tactics. On the basis of the name it was commonly given in the eighteenth-century, de Certeau calls the first variant, 'the science of fables', and the second, reflecting its ephemeral quality, the 'returns and turns of voices'. As I indicated above, these two variants represent two distinct branches of inquiry in a never completed research programme. What can be seen here, which I think is absolutely crucial to an understanding of de Certeau's work as a whole because of the analogical use he puts it to, is that both branches are connected to a single problem, the alienation of the voice by writing. By voice de Certeau really means the non-verbal cry of the body, something expressive without necessarily being articulate, a primitive resonance which as a matter of course language converts into phonemes, thus subordinating it to a machinic regime of expression, writing. However, writing is only the condition of possibility for this subordination of the body to the body-politic, as de Certeau puts it, not the actual instrument of its oppression (1984: 142). A writing-machine distinct from the text it inscribes and the parchment it inscribes on is needed for that purpose.[15] Voice refers then to whatever escapes this tripartite system of writing, writing-machine, and body.

The story of its alienation and subsequent return is the story of the advent and supersession of modernity. But beneath that story there subsists another story which, according to de Certeau, bespeaks a virtually immemorial struggle, of which modernity and postmodernity are but latter-day variant forms, and that is the inscription of laws on bodies (1984: 139). Between the body as page, and the collective body-politic as text, there exists an entire panoply of body-writing-machines, ranging from the primitive, such as tattoos and scarification, to the ultra-modern, like the barcode, which socialise the body by making it conform to a predetermined code or law: 'These tools compose a series of objects whose purpose is to inscribe the force of the law on its subject, to tattoo him [sic] in order to make him demonstrate the rule, to produce a "copy" that makes the norm legible' (de Certeau, 1984: 141). There is no law that is not inscribed on a body, de Certeau says, pointing to a logic still deeper in the cultural sediment than the one articulated in the account of the demise of orality (1984: 139). Even in a strictly oral economy laws are still inscribed on bodies, de Certeau observes, through initiation rites, circumcision, tattooing, scarification and so on, which is to say, the present attempt to subordinate the body to writing 'preceded the historical form that writing has taken in modern times' (1984: 139). And it is precisely that prior, more long-standing struggle, which de Certeau's schematisation of the relations between scriptural and oral economies is designed to bring into view. As such, his tripartite schema is really bipolar, or as Deleuze and Guattari (1987) put it, biunivocal: the body and the law, with the third element, the writing-machine, being consigned a purely mechanical role.

The body, de Certeau says, is effected by writing, by which we understand him to mean law not technology. On the one hand, 'living beings are "packed into a text" (in the sense that products are canned or packed), transformed into signifiers of rules (a sort of "intextuation") and, on the other hand, the reason or *Logos* of a society "becomes flesh" (an incarnation)' (de Certeau, 1984: 140). For the human sciences this presents an all but insoluble double-bind: in attempting to articulate the latter form, the way the concept body is made flesh in other words, it cannot help perpetuating the former practice, namely the blanket intextuation of voiceless, faceless others. In recognition of the inexorability of this theoretical and practical bind, de Certeau is only critical of scholarship that pretends not to rely on or practice intextuation; and in his own analyses he concentrates on the articulation of the means of escape from processes of incarnation. The theoretical implication is more interesting: it proposes both an essential body and a constructed body, as well as an essential effect of a socius which is itself completely constructivist. The cry alerts us to the persistence of a raw, essential body beneath the sediment of subjectification. The alienation of the voice and its persistence as a cry points to something deeper, more durable, than the subject underpinning de Certeau's discussion of culture, and that is the body.

The body is the baseline of de Certeau's thought, but nowhere does he provide an extensive account or theory of it, and for the most part, his interest in the body seems only to run skin deep. He is fascinated by tattoos and stigmata for instance, but not the viscera. The brief but scattered accounts of the body he does provide do suggest, however, that his underpinning theory of the body is in fact constructivist. What emerges from his analysis of the alienation of the voice by writing, though, is not the expected claim that the fundamental issue is the differing ways the other has been accommodated throughout history. No, something much more interesting becomes clear and that is that the other is itself but a response – or better, a solution – to a particular crisis, not a definitive and unchanging entity, and is accordingly subject to profound transformations which can be treated as registrations of epistemological movements. De Certeau's thesis, then, though never finally articulated, seems to be this: analysing how a culture responds to an epistemological crisis, is an efficient means of articulating the peculiar logic of that culture.

What we may wonder then is whether this applies today? In other words, can contemporary responses to alterity be used to define, or better, delineate the logic of postmodernity? Here I will take up as my signal example, Coetzee's *Foe* (1986), which for obvious reasons of continuity may enable us, against the background of *Robinson Crusoe*, to read this new logic of alterity. As an explicit and self-conscious attempt to rewrite or rework (or perhaps write back to) *Robinson Crusoe*, *Foe* needs to be read both for itself, as a novel in its own right, and as a contribution to a larger debate. What seems to me especially interesting about this novel is the way it manages to be these two things at once by writing its own story using the imaginative resources of another story. Quite literally, Coetzee makes *Foe* with the material

Robinson Crusoe provides, and the story itself reinforces this particular image of the writing-process: *Foe* uses Sue Barton's tale to write *Robinson Crusoe*, while Sue Barton uses Cruso's life story, and Friday's too, to enrich her own, which in turn she hopes will increase its sales. The issue that emerges here, one which is especially important to post-colonial studies today, is: who owns stories?[16] Who, moreover, has the right to trade or exchange stories? To profit from them, in other words. This issue is raised almost to crisis point when a postmodern perspective is taken on authorship (here I am referring more to a Hutcheon than a Jameson for my definition of postmodern). And indeed, it is in precisely such an undecidable milieu that *Foe* makes its intervention: what Coetzee is suggesting in this novel is that ownership of a story is immaterial besides the more critical issue of who tells the story.

By postmodern I mean a loss of the possibility of originality, which is articulated in two ways: (1) the limit on the number of stories that can be told; (2) the exhaustion of stylistic inflection and variation. Postmodernism, characteristically, has, instead of confronting this fact of the writing-process, celebrated it, and thereby subverted it. Rather than worry about originality, postmodern authors have turned a lack of originality into a feature of its style. What was once considered a lowly form of aesthetic achievement, suitable for apprentices perhaps, but otherwise marking as epigone any writer not able to rise above it, pastiche has today become a sign of literary sophistication and a marker of authenticity. It is worth noting, in this regard, that Coetzee has said of *Foe* that he hoped it was not pastiche, but acknowledges that it is one of the risks. His reason for this, I suspect, is that the premise of the novel is not in itself postmodern (if postmodern means mimesis without purpose), which is not to say, however, that it is actually modern.

Coetzee confronts all these obstacles to writing: the lack of new stories, the exhaustion of style, and so on. He begins with a story already told, and finds an untold story not behind, beneath or beside it, but before it. By postulating another storyteller besides Defoe, Coetzee is able to suppose that Defoe stylised his tale, which creates the possibility of reversal. And in rewriting *Robinson Crusoe* that is exactly what he did: he reversed Defoe's style, proving meanwhile that style is not exhausted. In interpolating a female storyteller, Coetzee proposes that the feminine persists in the telling of the tale, if not the tale itself. As such, he seems to be suggesting that self-assertion operates not in the words themselves, but in their actual expression. This is of course precisely the distinction de Certeau relies on in his elaboration of a politics of the weak. Briefly, I will try to show how Coetzee circumvents these three obstacles to writing, and the implications of his strategy.

First of all, then, Coetzee posits that *Robinson Crusoe* is an embellished tale, which is to say, someone else's story that has been digested and worked over by an artist, not solely the product of one man's imagination. Various literary historians have made speculations as to Defoe's source of inspiration, many pointing to contemporary shipwreck memoirs (Selkirk's being the most probable).[17] So this move does not in itself surprise us very much, as it is highly likely that there is a story *prior* to the one eventually published as *Robinson Crusoe*. Indeed, traditional literary historians assume that there is such a story, some going so far as to call it the 'real story'. But Coetzee, I suspect, was not much interested in any such thing as the real story of *Robinson Crusoe*, if by that one means an actual historical event. Rather his interest lay in the direction of the story of its actual writing, its stylisation. Initially, Sue Barton, like contemporary critics of history (Hayden White, Robert Nozick) and anthropology (James Clifford), worries that art will deprive her story of truth, but, in a crucial change of heart, later comes to realise that it is only through art the truth of her story can be captured.

Friday's tongueless mouth is, she thinks, the truth of her story, but obviously enough it is an unspeakable truth. Only art, therefore – in the sense Lyotard understands the term (as the necessary effort to present the unpresentable) – is capable of evoking this truth. What Coetzee is concerned with, then, is a politics of letters: art as the bearer of necessary truths, versus history as the dispassionate recorder of facts. The novel's enigmatic ending is, I think, an effort to evoke the sense of frustration any author mindful of the latter but earnest about the former must feel when trying to write. How does one convey a message through a story where one apparently cancels out the other? The greatest and most damnable form of silencing, Coetzee seems to say, is not the prohibition of free speech, but an apathetic audience. Sue Barton is thus saying: Friday has a voice, but we don't know how to hear it, and this is our shame. We expect him to speak, to say something, but all he does is dance in circles, cast petals on the waves, and stare dumbly at the sky. Because of the privilege given to exchange value by Western culture generally, but especially by the self-righteous utilitarians of Defoe's era, the symbolic value of Friday's self-expression is missed. Coetzee thus seems to follow Bakhtin (1981) in thinking that style is the creation of new voices. So through style the problem of a lack of voice, as felt by women and other minor voices, can be ameliorated. It is stylisation that creates the autonomous storyteller.

Notes

[1] A section of this chapter previously appeared in *New Blackfriars*, 77 (909): 483–93.

[2] According to Giard (1991a), the following three works by de Certeau can be thought of as 'heterological' in the strictest sense: de Certeau, 1980b; 1986: 67–79; 1988: 209–243.

[3] For a different, but not contradictory, account of the genealogy of de Certeau's notion of heterology see Colebrook, 1997: 130–4.

[4] 'God and the cannibal, equally elusive, are assigned by the text the role of the Word in whose name its writing takes place – but also the role of a place constantly altered by the inaccessible (t)exterior [*hor-texte*] which authorises that writing' (de Certeau, 1986: 68–9).

[5] For a critique of the inherent danger of Lyotard's notion that justice is only possible when judgements are made in the absence of previously determined criteria, see Norris, 1993: 86–8.

[6] 'We shall try to show that the *relation* between the same and the other ... is language. For language accomplishes a relation such that the terms are not limitrophe within this relation, such that the other, despite the relationship with the same, remains transcendent to the same. The relation between the same and other, metaphysics, is primordially enacted as a conversation ...' (Levinas, 1969: 39).

[7] 'Reality is always the plaintiff's responsibility' (Lyotard, 1988: 8).

[8] Not only does Derrida define justice in terms of an openness towards the other, he also defines deconstruction in these terms as well. 'Deconstruction', he says, 'is not an enclosure in nothingness [as a number of his detractors have alleged], *but an openness towards the other*' (Derrida, 1984: 124; my emphasis).

[9] According to Norris, Derrida takes this stance against Levinas in recognition of the fact that 'it is no great distance, whether in philosophic or in psychological terms, from the attitude that on principle renounces all claim to know or comprehend the other to the attitude that views otherness as a threat' (1994: 57).

[10] As Derrida puts it, empiricism 'has always been determined by philosophy, from Plato to Husserl, as *nonphilosophy*: as the philosophical pretension to nonphilosophy, the inability to justify oneself, to come to one's own aid as speech' (Derrida, 1978: 152).

[11] I have considered this last question at much greater length in Buchanan, 1998b.

[12] Its final shape would thus not be the one Augé offers of it in his own working through of the heterological problem (1998: 40). He reconciles the inner tension of the problem by eliminating the Same altogether: we are as other to ourselves, he argues, as we are to others, hence our relation to ourselves is no different from our relation to others.

[13] Umberto Eco's (1983 [1980]) *The Name of the Rose* offers a marvellous figuration of this shift by pitting an anachronistically modern, detective-figure (Brother William) who inquires into the authorship of signs, against a uninquiring group of Benedictine monks who assume all signs to be marks of God.

[14] 'The privilege of being himself the god that was formerly "separated" from his creation and defined by a *genesis* is transferred to the man shaped by enlightened culture' (de Certeau, 1984: 157).

[15] 'When there is no separation between the text to be inscribed and the body that historicises it, the system no longer functions. It is precisely the tools that establish that difference. They mark the gap without which everything becomes a disseminated writing, an indefinite combinative system of fictions and simulacra, or else, on the contrary, a continuum of natural forces, of libidinal drives and instinctual outpourings. Tools are the operators of writing and also its defenders' (de Certeau, 1984: 146).

[16] For a different, but sympathetic uptake of de Certeau as post-colonial critic, see Gregory, 1994.

[17] For an excellent account of the textual sources and inspirations of both Defoe's and Coetzee's texts, see Attridge, 1996.

5. Strategy and Tactics

> I prefer lucidity – perhaps a cruel lucidity – that seeks respectable
> authorities by beginning with an examination of real situations.
>
>   Michel de Certeau, *Culture in the Plural*

Strategy and tactics are undoubtedly de Certeau's most well known
concepts, yet for all their notoriety they remain poorly understood. Part
of the problem rests with de Certeau's own rather too thin formulation
of them in the first place, which is suggestive but not nearly as richly
argued and exampled as was really needed to make secure their
conceptual future.[1] In what follows, I will try to develop a fuller picture
of strategy and tactics by unpacking what I take to be their internal
logic, which I will try to show is dialectical rather than truly
polemological. Using a Greimasian model, I will argue that de
Certeau's fundamental conceptual move was to disenchain one (tactics)
from the other (strategy). In so doing the relation between them
becomes more contradictory than genuinely confrontational. A big part
of the problem de Certeau had with certain dismal trends he detected in
modern society stems from the fact that these two sorts of practices
really have ceased to communicate with another. But in disenchaining
strategy and tactics he created at least two blank spots in his schema
that need to be filled in if the whole thing is to hold together. Indeed,
the basic root cause of the subsequent misunderstandings and
enfeeblements of strategy and tactics as tools for cultural analysis arise
from a misperception of them as a binary pair (each being the logical
opposite of the other), built around a notion of power, when in reality
the picture is more complicated than that. In fact, it is truer to say they
offer an alternative to power as an organising model for understanding
society.

The other, bigger problem, is the basically anti-Foucauldian
atmosphere in which strategy and tactics found favour, which insofar as
it was really a discipline-wide abreaction to any and all systemic or
totalising theories of power could be stretched to include a host of
positions not specifically embraced by Foucault, indeed some of them,
such as Marxism, explicitly rejected by him.[2] By the same token,
Foucault's (1978: 95) assertion that wherever power is to be found

resistance will also be found demanded some new classification of the position that used to be known as the disempowered or the powerless and tactics seemed to fit the bill. So even the pro-Foucault camp found reason to be interested in de Certeau's model, however mistaken such a correspondence turns out to be. In the hands of John Fiske (1988), for instance, de Certeau was to become a theorist of the little victories of daily life, which were in themselves treated as somehow revolutionary, albeit on a minor scale.[3] Critics of this position, such as John Frow (1991; 1992) and Meaghan Morris (1990), were quick to point out, and rightly, that a meaningful politics of cultural change can hardly be based on so weak a foundation as the glancing blows Fiske catalogued as 'little victories'. Thus, the very thing that had originally seemed so appealing in de Certeau's theory, namely the possibility of theorising daily life in terms of empowerment in an upbeat rather than defeatist fashion, proved to be the very thing that led more level-headed critics to reject it. My own position (Buchanan, 1997) has always been that such a rejection is overhasty and that de Certeau is not nearly so frivolous as some of his followers, like Fiske, but there are others as well, would make it seem. And anyway as I will argue here, strategy and tactics are not so much modalities of power as indexes of belief.

Let me start, then, by reading into the record, as it were, the crucial passages in which de Certeau announces and defines these two terms: 'I call a *strategy* the calculation (or manipulation) of power relationships that becomes possible as soon as a subject with will and power (a business, an army, a city, a scientific institution) can be isolated. It postulates a *place* that can be delimited as its *own* and serve as the base from which relations with an *exteriority* composed of targets or threats (customers or competitors, enemies, the country surrounding the city, objectives and objects of research, etc.) can be managed' (de Certeau, 1984: 35–6). The essential point to observe, of course, is that strategy is a function of place, yet it takes a certain kind of strategic thinking or operating to actually produce a place. This biunivocality, which as we shall see is present in tactics as well, is doubtless both the most intriguing aspect of de Certeau's logic of practices and the most confusing, or at any rate least transparent. 'By contrast with a strategy (whose successive shapes introduce a certain play into this formal schema and whose link with a particular historical configuration of rationality should also be clarified), a *tactic* is a calculation determined by the absence of a proper locus. No delimitation of an exteriority, then, provides it with the condition necessary for autonomy. The space of the tactic is the space of the other' (de Certeau, 1984: 36–7). The common denominator, which we shall have to reckon with more fully in what follows, is the fact they are both determined as *calculations*.

In choosing to centre his attention on strategy and tactics de Certeau rejected several then and still prominent models of cultural analysis (structuralism and psychoanalysis being only the two most noted). He made it his particular brief to find a way of grasping the 'timing' of the various cultural activities that scholars of popular culture had hitherto catalogued, but in the process museumified, that is, rendered both inert and timeless. De Certeau's signal example is the proverb. Aarne's and Propp's analyses of proverbs, distinct as they are from one another, both treat proverbs as a type of content to be collected and divided into units. These units and the relations between them can then be used either to map the 'mental geography peculiar to a given group' as Aarne did, or determine the 'modes of production' of proverbs, which was the path taken by Propp (de Certeau, 1984: 20). 'Through a twofold control of the corpus they circumscribe and of the operations they carry out on it, these methods succeed in defining their object themselves (what is a proverb?), in rationalising its collection, in classifying the types and transforming the "given" into something reproducible (for example, if one knows the rules of the production of proverbs, one can fabricate series of them). These techniques thus provide, by explaining them, the ability to *construct* social phenomena, just as biology synthesises insulin' (de Certeau, 1984: 20). The message is of course that life is not a laboratory experiment, therefore our means of analysing it should not turn it into one.

For more or less the same reason, Lévi-Strauss's structuralist model is seen to be just as problematic by de Certeau. Indeed, in his view, it is little different from either Propp's formalism or Aarne's typologism, which inasmuch as it uses content as so much fodder for the elucidation of form is probably a fair if not nuanced comment: 'The drawback of this method, which is at the same time the condition of its success, is that it extracts the documents from their *historical* context and eliminates the *operations* of speakers in particular situations of time, place, and competition' (de Certeau, 1984: 20). In order to grasp something so elusive as the content of daily life, the various formal approaches to it felt they had to sacrifice certain aspects of it, the main one being its situational logic. Of course, sociology, anthropology and ethnology have since become vastly more sophisticated so a lot of what de Certeau complains of with respect to his own contemporaries probably no longer applies. Even his specific charges against Bourdieu need to be tempered in the light of permutations in his work in the quarter century since de Certeau made them. Still, the thrust of his argument remains fresh; a fact that can be witnessed in the work of Haraway (1991) and Clifford (1988) who both continue to grapple with the same issues de Certeau raised, namely the difficulty of articulating the logic of culture in a way that does not assume it to be cadaverous. What de Certeau wanted to introduce into the equation was some means of articulating the specific uses cultural contents are put to. In what instances does one use a proverb? When is it appropriate to do so, and why?

> Like tools, proverbs (and other discourses) are *marked by* uses; they offer to analysis the *imprints of acts* or of processes of enunciation; they signify the *operations* whose object they have been, operations which are relative to situations and which can be thought of as the conjunctural *modalisations* of statements or of practices; more generally, they thus indicate a social *historicity* in which systems of representations or processes of fabrication no longer appear only as normative frameworks but also as *tools manipulated by users*. (de Certeau, 1984: 21)

Just as importantly, as we will explore in the next chapter, these two types of calculation embody the logic of the type of spatiality they issue from: strategy is a technique of place, and tactics is a technique of space. The essential difference between the two is the way they relate to the variables that everyday life inevitably throws at us all. Strategy works to limit the sheer number of variables affecting us by creating some kind of protected zone, a place in which the environment can be rendered predictable if not properly tame. This is why *Robinson Crusoe* is the example par excellence of strategic thinking: as we've seen, Crusoe's actions are almost entirely motivated by defensive thoughts of this kind. He is paranoid and he works through his paranoia by building castles. One can say the same of virtually all the disciplinary procedures catalogued by Foucault: they too are paranoid, but they work through their paranoia by domesticating the body itself. By rendering the body docile, they arrest in advance the very impulse to rebellion. Tactics, by contrast, is the approach one takes to everyday life when one is unable to take measures against its variables. Tactics are constantly in the swim of things and are as much in danger of being swept away or submerged by the flow of events as they are capable of bursting through the dykes strategy erects around itself and suffusing its protected place with its own brand of subversive and incalculable energy. Tactics refers to the set of practices that strategy has not been able to domesticate. They are not in themselves subversive, but they have a symbolic value which is not to be underestimated: they offer daily proof of the partiality of strategic control and in doing so they hold out the token hope that however bad things get, they are not *necessarily* so. In other words, tactics operate primarily on the plane of belief.

This is true of even that most notorious of cases offered by de Certeau, *la perruque* (easily his most misunderstood and maligned supporting example).[4] '*La perruque* is the worker's own work disguised as work for his employer. It differs from pilfering in that nothing of material value is stolen. It differs from absenteeism in that the worker is officially on the job. *La perruque* may be as simple a matter as a secretary's writing a love letter on "company time" or as complex as a cabinetmaker's "borrowing" a lathe to make a piece of furniture for his living room' (de Certeau, 1984: 25). The worker has no compunction about stealing time because he or she does not believe in the job he or she is performing – it is no longer a vocation in the old sense of being a calling, it is merely that which one does in order to pay the bills. The fact is, de Certeau adds, whatever you choose to call it, this practice is on the increase and not only in France: it is a global phenomenon: 'With variations practices analogous to *la perruque* are proliferating in governmental and commercial offices as well as in factories' (de Certeau, 1984: 26). The point is that *la perruque* is not an exemplary instance of tactics in action so much as a symptom of a broader problem, one which, moreover, de Certeau seems prepared to give an epochal character. And that indeed is how we should understand tactics: as a symptom of postmodernity. De Certeau doesn't use that word of course, but it fits with his diagnoses. Inasmuch as tactics reflect changes in work practices they can also be taken to be symptomatic of deeper changes in the mode of production itself.

De Certeau's definitions of strategy and tactics are, by now, quite famous, judging by the sheer number of times they have been cited. However, in all but very few cases, these citations drop de Certeau's essential framing remarks, his expressions of hesitancy and so on, which scrupulously position strategy and tactics as the product of a preliminary hypothesis. After rejecting 'trajectory' as unsuited to the conceptual needs of the problem at hand – namely, the ongoing task of finding an adequate language to represent a 'living culture' – de Certeau candidly states that a 'distinction between *strategies* and *tactics* appears to provide a more adequate initial schema' (1984: 35). We must also make mention of yet another aspect of de Certeau's frame that tends to be neglected and that is the fact that no later verification of this particular 'preliminary hypothesis' is ever supplied; it is and remains a tentative suggestion awaiting proper and full concretisation. We know from Giard's history of the research project which culminated in the publication of the two volumes of *The Practice of Everyday Life* that a third volume was planned, so perhaps it had been intended that the final realisation of these concepts should be left until then. Alas, as we now know, no such third volume ever got written. My implication is that while it is true that one cannot help using strategy and tactics in a context other than their own, on first reading one must try to develop them in dialogue with the larger project they initially formed a part. My job here will be to elucidate that larger project.

To that end, let me underscore what I see as the pivotal hypothesis of *The Practice of Everyday Life*, namely the view that the everyday evidences a discernible form and conceals a knowable logic. That being said, we must also acknowledge the fact that the limited aim of *The*

Practice of Everyday Life was simply to make a certain type of discussion possible, not to broach that discussion and carry it to its conclusions. For this reason, we should forgive its lack of detail and read it in the suggestive spirit it was intended.[5] So, while there can be no question that it is a tentative, searching work, not a polished, conclusive one, that is not to say it doesn't sparkle with important and interesting ideas. Yet this is not how most critics have approached it and, accordingly, it has tended to be perceived (unjustly, in my view) as a failed though admirable attempt to do something different within the constrained field of the human sciences (Frow, 1991). However, this is not an assessment we need accept. My position is that in spite of the growing attention de Certeau's work is currently receiving we still do not know what his theory is capable of and we will never know unless we approach it from the perspective of his overall project.[6] In what follows, I will offer a schematic description of the overall project as well as an image of its underlying 'ethic' or rationale.

Although he is often accused of writing in a slippery, fugitive style (not without justification, I might add), de Certeau could not be more explicit in stating his aims. *The Practice of Everyday Life* is, he states, 'part of a continuing investigation of the ways in which users – commonly assumed to be passive and guided by established rules – operate' (de Certeau, 1984: xi). Its aim 'is not so much to discuss this elusive yet fundamental subject as to make such a discussion possible; that is, by means of inquiries and hypotheses, to indicate pathways for future' (de Certeau, 1984: xi). The measure of the success of the project will be whether or not the practices of everyday life remain in the background or not, whether, in other words, their specificity of operation is delineated and articulated, or not. The focus here, de Certeau thoughtfully emphasises, is on practices, not subjects; as such, his investigations imply neither a return to a liberal humanist concern for the individual nor a reiteration of the structuralist interest in the production of discourses. Neither an enunciating subject, nor a subject of enunciation, occupy the first position in de Certeau's scheme: that honour is reserved for enunciation, or, to put it another way, it is the modality of practices, which, in reality, is the true subject of his inquiry. As de Certeau himself puts it, 'the question at hand concerns modes of operation or schemata of action, and not directly the subjects (or persons) who are their authors or vehicles' (1984: xi). It is equally invalid, then, to say, as Morris (1990) does, that de Certeau privileges the ordinary man at the expense of the ordinary woman, as it is to say that he concentrates overmuch on the other (whether defined as woman, black, gay or Jew), since neither are his actual objects of inquiry, but merely effects of what he is really trying to specify, namely the operational logic of culture.

Although it is never announced as such, de Certeau's method is dialectical: the minutiae of everyday life are to be brought into view by way of their underpinning logic, which is at once invisible and presupposed.[7] It is also dialectical in a political sense too, which I will use Greimas's square to bring out more fully below. It is the development of a notion of cultural logic that enables de Certeau to realise his plan of moving more or less insignificant cultural practices such as cooking and walking into the foreground of critical attention. As it is this never fully specified logic that is supposed to account for the contrary view of culture that de Certeau hopes to present by rendering logical, albeit still paradoxical, such apparently aberrant ideas as the power of the powerless, the activity of the passive, the productions of non-producers, escaping without leaving and so on, it is precisely that which should be the focus of our attention. Accepting the basic state of incompletion of de Certeau's overall project is no impediment to this line of inquiry since his blueprints are quite clear on how exactly this logic was to be derived. Indeed, in view of the fact that they describe the limits and aims of the project they could be said to initiate it. By the same token, as I have tried to show throughout, de Certeau's work is animated by a quest which Geldof rightly characterises as the search for a conceptual framework, or logic if you will, capable of addressing the everyday as both ordinary and other (1997: 32).

So, how did de Certeau propose to derive a logic of culture? His first move is, as he called it, a negative one (de Certeau, 1984: xii). He rules out any focus on the production of cultural difference by counter-culture groups both because it is obvious and has been done before, but also because such productions are in his view merely symptoms or indexes of deeper complexities. Like Deleuze, de Certeau's interest is not in the production of difference, but different productions, a fact which seems to have escaped many of even his most enthusiastic supporters who, in cultural studies at least, deploy his ideas to valorise such trivial subversions as wearing jeans (Fiske, 1989). This becomes obvious when we examine his three so-called positive determinations. To begin with, de Certeau proposes to combine two lines of inquiry that had hitherto been kept in a kind of quarantine from one another, namely the study of what, broadly speaking, may be referred to as cultural representations (T-shirts fully as much as films, books and shopping malls) on the one hand, and the study of modes of behaviour on the other (what one in fact does with these representations). What he had in mind, though, was not merely the combination of textual analysis and behavioural analysis (a convergence that today is practically a commonplace), but rather their synthesis.

> For example, the analysis of the images broadcast by television (representation) and of the time spent watching television should be

complemented by a study of what the cultural consumer 'makes' or 'does' during this time and with these images. (de Certeau, 1984: xii)

The same applies to the use of space, de Certeau goes on to suggest, as well as commodities purchased in supermarkets, even newspaper and magazine stories could be so regarded. De Certeau defines this 'making' as a *poiesis* whose chief characteristic is its lack of visibility. It is a hidden production because it takes places in fields already defined and occupied by large production-systems (television, urban development etc.) which according to a logic of scale tend to swamp the non-systemic with their outputs, and because there is no place where this *other* production could actually exhibit itself (1984: xii). There is no place to look for this production, then, except where by definition it cannot be seen. The difficulties do not end there. The task of articulating this *other* production is made even more frustrating by the fact that it does not manifest itself in products as such, 'but rather through its *ways of using* the products imposed by a dominant economic order' (de Certeau, 1984: xiii). Literally, then, this mode of production produces nothing but itself, but does not even have an 'itself' to show for its efforts, however great or small they may be. Such a production therefore cannot be said to be symbolic, but neither can it be said to be unreal or purely imaginary.

The second positive determination is inspired by Foucault's *Discipline and Punish*. De Certeau is famously ambivalent about this book. He cannot but admire the deft way Foucault reorganises an existing field of inquiry along new lines. As de Certeau puts it, 'instead of analysing the apparatus exercising power (i.e., the localisable, expansionist, repressive, and legal institutions), Foucault analyses the mechanisms (*dispositifs*) that have sapped the strength of these institutions and surreptitiously reorganised the functioning of power' (1984: xiv). In this way, Foucault has made possible a much richer, and much more fluid understanding of the way power suffuses every aspect of social life, from the way we comport our bodies to the laws we observe. Perhaps most importantly, Foucault offers a productivist notion of power in contrast to the then prevailing repressive conceptions of power (Marcuse, Reich, Brown). But despite raising new and interesting questions about the way power operates, it 'privileges the productive apparatus (which produces the "discipline")' (de Certeau, 1984: xiv) at the expense of the productions of the people it supposedly disciplines. Such productions are repressed by discipline, or better, redirected, which is the central job of education after all. Yet to repress is not to eradicate, something psychoanalysis at once explains and is premised on. Therefore, the truism that discipline has insinuated itself into every facet of daily life needs to be balanced against the fact that the everyday has not been reduced to a rigid set of regimes such as the notion of discipline implies.[8] So, rather than extend its analyses into new fields but along the same lines, what de Certeau proposes to do is explore the obverse side of Foucault's analyses, looking not for patterns of resistance, which Foucault postulates anyway, but subtle movements of escape and evasion. What Foucault's system lacks, in de Certeau's assessment, which he then sets out to remedy himself, is an adequate account of authority, the true obverse of power.

De Certeau's reply to Foucault, as we might characterise it, takes the form of a separation of power and authority. While these terms may variously be thought as functions of each other – power giving rise to authority, or the reverse – this does not mean they are in fact one and the same thing. On the contrary, de Certeau argues that they should be viewed as supplementary: where one was the other shall be. The 'old powers', as de Certeau calls the pre-disciplinary regimes, used to compensate their lack of technical proficiency in social control with a clever manipulation of their authority. Before the advent of the panopticon, power was maintained through the creation of systems of debt, affiliation and allegiance. But since this system was enormously uncertain, prone as it was to the intrigues of adventurers and pretenders, the 'old powers' constantly worked at freeing themselves from the intolerable fluctuations of fidelity through a rationalisation of space and control: 'As the result of this labour, the powers in our developed societies have at their disposal rather subtle and closely-knit procedures for the control of all social networks: these are the administrative and "panoptic" procedures of the police, the schools, health services, security, etc. But they are slowly losing all credibility. They have more power and less authority' (de Certeau, 1984: 179). And that is the rub, as far as de Certeau is concerned, panopticism has steadily eroded the aura of authority the previous regimes cloaked themselves in and in the process has brought about a generalised routing of credulity itself.

Here, then, several years before Lyotard (1984 [first published in French in 1979]) made his cataclysmic pronouncement that postmodernism had arrived and that it is characterised by a growing incredulity towards apparatuses of cultural legitimation, the metanarratives of religion, progress and history, and the like, de Certeau had already diagnosed the source of the rot his colleague and countless others after him would so piously lament: the evaporation of belief.[9] Written in the cool aftermath of those all too hot days of May 1968, de Certeau's reflections on the impact of the shattering of the authority of the powers that were (which we discussed in Chapter 2), seem to have gotten progressively gloomier. From the rosy hopefulness of their first flush, when he was prepared to believe anything was possible, de Certeau's responses to the ongoing cultural revolution initiated in that infamously long month became less and less hopeful as the years wore on. By 1974 he was declaring that his solidarity could only be with those goodly souls working towards the creation of new kinds of authority and not those who would continue to denounce any and all forms of authority.

> They have the courage to see and to say what they see; they justly refuse to mistake mountains for molehills (to mistake for 'authorities' the powers and traditions that merely *use* what they are supposed to *represent*); they are opposed to the demeaning therapeutics that anaesthetise a society, that are in collusion with an irresponsibility in order to profit it from it, and that exploit a discontent for immediate gain, whose broader implications are only too predictable. (de Certeau, 1997b: 4)

We know that, in his last years, de Certeau was preparing a plan for an extended work on what he called 'heterology'. A major part of this proposed study was going to be an anthropology of belief (Giard, 1991a: 212). He wanted to investigate both its actual instantiation and its abstract quality as a practice that needs Gods – or, it might be better to say, lacks them – rather than one that emanates from God as original cause. Some of the key arguments for this work are announced in the last chapters of *The Practice of Everyday Life* where de Certeau enacts the crucial separation of belief as an act or cultural practice from the thing believed in. 'As a first approximation,' belief is, he says, 'the subject's investment in a proposition, the *act* of saying it and considering it as true' (de Certeau, 1984: 178) and not a particular content, dogma or programme. What I am suggesting now is that de Certeau's arguments with Foucault only take on their full signifiance in light of this larger project. The aim of this investigation was not, however, to demonstrate the inherent mobility of belief, but to find out how it came to be so free-floating in the first place. In other words, de Certeau's investigations are provoked by the evident fact that today God no longer alone commands belief. Nowadays, one is just as likely to believe in the miraculously deep penetrating action of a new kitchen cleanser as God. The mobility of belief is seen by de Certeau as symptomatic of a deeper social ill, namely the erosion of what he called 'authority'. Authority, de Certeau says, signifies 'a reality that is difficult to determine, but nonetheless necessary: the air that allows a society to breathe' (1997b: 3).

Belief is mobile because authority is lacking. Lyotard's (1984) rather abysmal claim that nowadays not even metanarratives like History and Progress and so on are able to hold us fast anymore is simply an extension of the same point because these things actually stand in the place of God in a secularised, or what Kant called Enlightened, society. This is in effect what Nietzsche meant by saying man killed God: we replaced Him with a series of pretenders, none of which have ever attained quite His status in our eyes hence our powerful disposition towards incredulity. We are disappointed in our own sad inventions and consequently remain constantly on the look out for more favourable substitutes. To de Certeau's way of thinking, though, this process had gotten out of hand by the late 1960s and early 1970s (though God knows the rot had set in long before) when it seemed we were prepared to start believing in the pre-packaged wisdom of advertising because the other apparatuses – God, reason and so forth – had been so thoroughly discredited. Yet, tellingly, de Certeau does not counsel a greater scepticism, although he does call for a sharper lucidity, which would give up on belief altogether.

> The sickness of confidence, the doubt in respect to political apparatuses and representations (whether monetary or unionised), and the successive forms of a lingering discontent now recall for us this element that is forgotten in times of certainty and that appears indispensable only when it is lacking or rotting away. But must we conclude that, without air, everything would be for the best, that, without authorities, society would be free from all this discontent? It would be tantamount to attending to the death of the patient instead of curing his or her illness. (de Certeau, 1997b: 3)

The third positive determination is the assumption that the practices of everyday life must conceal a logic of their own, which may go back to primitive times. Such an idea is of course already enshrined in the aforementioned suggestion that cultural practices might be articulated by recourse to a notion of syntax. Here though it is not simply a matter of articulating an elusive set of phenomena by superimposing a grid, an approach already made standard by structuralism anyway; rather it is saying that the practices themselves are conditioned by this grid, a still structuralist idea to be sure, but differing in one very important respect. Now instead of saying that subjects obey an internalised logic they can neither know nor evade, de Certeau is saying cultural logic is like a menu from which subjects choose already worked-out actions according to their perceived needs. Hence their correlation to narrative, a connection de Certeau makes more explicit in relation to spatiality (as we will see in the next chapter). Insofar as those actions are adopted and personalised, they form a repertoire, which is as close to a habitus as de Certeau is prepared to go. In order to grasp this logic, de Certeau undertakes two types of investigations: on the one hand, he tries his hand at description, initiating a language experiment, and on the other hand, an examination of a range of possible hypotheses. Overall the problem is how to articulate a set of productive practices that produce nothing and therefore must seem illusory without turning them into something they are not, a set of hollow symbols. This allows him to develop his science of singularity along the lines of what Jameson has called a semiotics of modality.

The principle benefit of a modal semiotics, and de Certeau's primary achievement in the elaboration of such a system, is its deconstruction of the phenomenological divide between foreground practices and background practices which, in philosophy and history at least, has led to a profound neglect of the ordinary activities of daily life in favour of so-called higher functions like political thought, art and so on. His immediate methodological aim – which we must now try to place in its proper ideological light – will be realised, he goes on to say, when a theory of the everyday capable of articulating it in its specificity is devised. Then, and only then, de Certeau seems to think, everyday practices, no matter how insignificant or superficial, will cease to appear as the obscure background of social activity (1984: xi). As can plainly be seen, there is no question in de Certeau's mind that the everyday does exist. His starting point is not whether a set of background practices can be adduced, but whether an indeterminate set of largely unremarkable activities – newly labelled as 'practices', by de Certeau, and collectively described as 'the everyday' – can first of all be rendered less dense, and second raised sufficiently in status to capture the attention of social scientists with eyes for foreground practices only.[10] Here we get another glimpse of the dystopian hue which washes over his entire oeuvre. Confirmation of our suspicion is found a few pages later on when de Certeau offers this stunning clarification of his purpose: 'An investigation analogous to Chomsky's study of the oral uses of language *must seek to restore* to everyday practices their logical and cultural legitimacy, at least in the sectors – still very limited – in which we have at our disposal the instruments necessary to account for them' (de Certeau, 1984: xvi; my emphasis). It is dystopian because its premise is that somehow past actions have betrayed the present.

The goal of de Certeau's study is only superficially comparable to that of contemporary cultural studies – this is true whether we compare his work to his Anglo-American contemporaries of the 1970s, notably the Birmingham school, or our present day thinkers in this field, such as John Frow, Lawrence Grossberg and Meaghan Morris. In contrast to the work of people like Stuart Hall and the other pioneers of what we today know as cultural studies, de Certeau's goal was never to develop a theoretical apparatus capable of both articulating the more mundane features of the everyday in their concrete – which is to say denaturalised and political – specificity, and legitimating such an enterprise in the sceptical eyes of traditional scholarship. Unlike the current trend among cultural studies thinkers, de Certeau did not interest himself in the politics of identity, or anything that smacked of what he saw as an egregious return to a politics of individuality. Indeed, like Deleuze, de Certeau's interest was rather in the impersonal, the non-individual, that which spoke through the individual subject, rather than what he or she thought or had to say. He wanted to contrive an analysis of culture from the mute perspectives of the body, the cry, and the murmur, none of which needs to be identified with a specific, knowable individual, in order to be apprehended. So for de Certeau, it was never merely a matter of authorising the study of the everyday in its particulars that he had it in mind for his newly inaugurated science to do. Much more boldly, he aimed at the legitimation of the everyday itself as a resource for the primordial understanding of human behaviour.

The articulation of this primordial understanding of human behaviour would, de Certeau supposed, take the form of a *combinatoire*. Its model, he speculated, 'may go as far back as the age-old ruses of fishes and insects that disguise or transform themselves in order to survive, and which has in any case been concealed by the form of rationality currently dominant in Western culture' (de Certeau, 1984: xi). Unfortunately, in formulating this *combinatoire*, de Certeau did not get beyond the stage of the initial hypothesis that the twin concepts of strategy and tactics might serve his purpose. What I propose to do now is take this hypothesis to the next stage, which is the elaboration of the *combinatoire* itself. By utilising Greimas's (1987) concept of the semiotic rectangle or square I hope to lay to rest the lingering misapprehension that strategy and tactics are a dualism, and show instead that they refer to a fundamental contradiction in our culture. In this regard, I will rely on Jameson's (1987: xiv–xv; 1972: 162–9) dialectical usage of Greimas, which hinges on the fact that Greimas's model is able to transform any binary into at least ten positions, and by so doing develop what we might call a cognitive map of a certain way of narrating cultural practice. And while this obviously explodes the idea that a binary is only ever a matter of two opposing sides, it also turns out to be a very effective means of articulating the underpinning ideology of a theoretical construction. It exposes the relations between abstract units the narrative process would normally submerge, it being part and parcel of the storytelling process itself to complicate as much and as deeply as possible all relations.

As the better Hitchcock films demonstrate, and contemporary action films exploit to the nth degree, the thrill in a thriller is not contained in the moment of discovery at the end, namely the revelation of whodunnit, but in the ongoing failure on the part of the audience and hero alike to re-establish the set of relations that make sense of what takes place at the level of plot. It is not enough to know why A killed B, never mind the dull fact that A did kill B, rather we want to know from what point of view it makes sense for A to kill B. Sadly this has now been reified in the form of the serial killer movie (*Silence of the Lambs, Copycat, Seven* and *Kiss the Girls*, to name only a few of the more notable examples) which elaborates an entire aesthetics of murder based on the idea that sense can be found in even the most twisted actions providing its unique world view can be reconstructed. My point is that

Greimas does not merely identify the heroes and villains, to put it crudely, he also unlocks the logical schema that impels them towards one another in a way they cannot avoid. As viewers we do all that we can to avoid asking what the narrative relation between the killer and the detective is, and yet this is where the ideology of such movies is really to be found. A similar relation obtains between a theorist and the concepts he or she uses.

Greimas's sturdy and deeply structuralist conviction is that narrative is itself a way of thinking, a mode of cognition in other words, and is therefore susceptible to the same precise, algorithmic analyses structuralists have endeavoured to produce for kinship studies, philosophy, mathematics and the sciences in general. It is a two-way street, however, as Jameson has pointed out, because while it transforms narratives 'back into something that still distantly resembles a cognitive dynamic' it also opens the already overtly cognitive texts – like philosophy, mathematics and the sciences – to narrative analysis (1987: xii). In this respect, the Greimassian square is something of a unified field theory for the social sciences; and while I am duly suspicious of it for precisely this reason, it is still a very useful means of mapping at once the terms of de Certeau's analyses, his reasons for using those particular terms, and his purpose in doing so.

Jameson offers the following advice for the construction of Greimassian squares, which I have found very helpful. There are, he says, three crucial operative moments in the actual manufacture of the square, and one must be prepared to blacken a lot of working-out paper before getting it right. The first concerns the choice of terms themselves, in this case strategy and tactics, and equally importantly, the order in which they are to be presented in the square – tactics on the left and strategy on the right, or strategy on the left and tactics on the right? The significance of this latter decision can probably only be seen once the square is actually put together, but Jameson's point that it refers to the temporality of the square not its spatiality is worth bearing in mind. The left and right sides are already figures for dominant and subordinate, centre and periphery, and so on, so it is obvious that the positioning of terms is going to be crucial in a symbolic sense; the temporality of this decision comes into play as the square is expanded and the question of change is taken into consideration. The second recommendation Jameson makes is to conceive the four primary terms in the square as polysemically as possible, thus allowing the full range of synonyms to be brought into play, and thereby prevent what he elsewhere describes as the danger of premature clarification. For our purposes this means finding synonyms for strategy and tactics which is anything but easy. However, it does serve the extremely useful and interesting function of breaking these terms out of their militarist closet, creating some astonishingly productive connections in the process.

The third and final piece of advice Jameson offers comes in the form
of a warning. The fourth term, the negation of the negation, must be, if
the square is successful, 'the place of novelty and paradoxical
emergence' (1987: xvi). On this point I can only say that the proof will
be in the pudding. Let us now turn to the construction of the square
itself. The first two terms of the binary, strategy and tactics, are to be
designated as S1 and S2. The significance of this is that from the outset
they are not conceived as structurally opposite, or antithetical, but as
different. Strategy should not be thought of as the negation of tactics in
other words, nor tactics as the negative side of strategy, rather the
relationship between them is one of contradiction. And this is how we
generate the next two terms in the square: by adding the genuine
negations of strategy and tactics, which will be designated as S1' and
S2'. The square is composed then of two sets of contradictory terms and
two sets of negative terms, which means there are four relations to be
considered, two horizontals and two diagonals: between S1 and S2, and
between S1 and S1', plus S2 and S2' as well as between S1' and S2'
(Jameson, 1987: xiv). See Figure 5.1 for how the square looks.

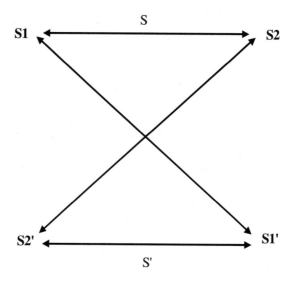

Figure 5.1

The question now is how to fill in the blanks. I will suggest that strategy
should occupy the first position (S1) and tactics the second (S2) for the
simple reason that strategy does indeed dominate tactics and this is
therefore the proper representation of their relationship. Now comes the
interesting part: what negates strategy? And what negates tactics?

Negation is of course a rather tricky term, so by way of clarification, I will say that by negation I mean the process whereby what was once in the foreground is somehow forced into the background and made to serve the secondary function of pointing-up the new term. The term 'postmodernism' is, it seems to me, a classic example of how this works: in Lyotard's (1984) case, for instance, modernism remains the indispensable benchmark, not merely as the true measure of postmodernism's authenticity and/or originality, both of which are of course hotly disputed, but far more crucially as that which gives meaning to its prefix. It will be only slightly misleading if I say what I am looking for now is something that may fairly be classified as post-strategy and post-tactics (it is misleading because of the suggestion that negation is a matter of succession, which it is not, but not invalid). It should also be observed that I am modifying Greimas somewhat by using negation instead of simple negatives like non-strategy and non-tactics. My reason for doing so, which I hope excuses the distortion, is that the problem I wish to solve using the Greimassian square is precisely one of transition: I am interested in the dissolution of strategy and the hardening of tactics, both of which eventualities or developments are frequently alluded to by de Certeau but never explored. His only clue is that tactics introduce a Brownian motion into strategy, which besides suggesting that tactics reinvigorate strategy is hardly very satisfying.

Insofar as tactics is concerned, its negation, which is the very term we were warned about, is likely to cause a bit of trouble. As for strategy, an answer may already be at hand. Given that for de Certeau strategy is the force at work in the production of what Foucault called discipline, whatever follows Foucault's panopticism, in an epochal sense, might justly be thought of as post-strategy and fit the bill. The obvious and I believe correct choice here is Deleuze's notion of the society of control, which is explicitly conceived as *post*-panoptic.[11] 'We're in the midst of a general breakdown of all sites of confinement – prisons, hospitals, factories, schools, the family. ... It's simply a matter of nursing them through their death throes and keeping people busy until the new forces start knocking at the door to take over. *Control societies* are taking over from disciplinary societies' (Deleuze, 1995: 178; emphasis in original). The difference between the two, the illumination of which – according to Deleuze – was Foucault's point all along, is this: 'Control is short-term and rapidly shifting, but at the same time continuous and unbounded, whereas discipline was long-term, infinite, and discontinuous. A man is no longer a man confined but a man in debt' (Deleuze, 1995: 181). As an apparatus of control, it cannot be chaos (my code-word for tactics, and the apparent opposite of control) that negates strategy. Chaos is what one endeavours to control using such techniques as strategy puts at our disposal; it is not, and by definition cannot be, the negative of control (it would be like saying the stockwhip is the negative of cattle), rather it is its everlasting contradiction. The true negative of strategy is another mode of control, not tactics.

As to the matter of the negative of tactics, I will go out on a limb here and suggest that Jameson's concept of the 'cultural revolution' is the best available choice, it being an extrapolation of precisely the same set of concerns de Certeau's inquiry into May 1968 set out to investigate only on a global scale. It refers to 'that moment in which the coexistence of various modes of production becomes visibly antagonistic, their contradictions moving to the very centre of political, social, and historical life' (Jameson, 1981: 95). For instance, 'Western Enlightenment may be grasped as part of a properly bourgeois cultural revolution, in which the values and discourses, the habits and daily space, of the *ancien régime* were systematically dismantled so that in their place could be set the new conceptualities, habits and life forms, and value systems of a capitalist market society' (Jameson, 1981: 96).[12] But it is not as a new name for transition that Jameson intends cultural revolution; rather he uses it to estrange the very notion of transition itself. Transitional moments are but passages to the surface, Jameson suggests (1981: 97), of deeper and perhaps primordial processes in human society; their moment of triumph is always to be kept in the perspective of an eternal struggle and never to be allowed to be treated as in anyway permanent.

In the context of de Certeau's work, I use the term 'cultural revolution' to describe the paradoxically 'bureaucratic' process by which some nonconformist movements pursue their anarchic aims. As de Certeau puts it, 'every reformist power is tempted to acquire political advantages, to transform itself into an ecclesiastical administration in order to support its project, to thus lose its primitive "purity" or change it into a mere decoration of the apparatus, and to transform its militants into officials or conquerors' (1984: 184). It will have been noticed, no doubt, that my modification of Greimas caters to precisely this point: it introduces a state of perpetual struggle into what could otherwise become a static 'kodak moment', with all the attendant ironies of reification that implies (I might add, this is my suggestion for how de Certeau's rubric polemology might be rendered semiotically). The relationship between tactics and strategy is akin to that of the logic of the reversal of *shi* in Chinese thought, but as I've just asserted it has an inherent agency that Chinese thought does not have because it banks on propensity. Thus the Chinese model is exactly a snapshot of the relation between strategy and tactics, not an explanation: 'On the one hand, every tendency, once born, is naturally inclined to grow; on the other hand, any tendency carried to its ultimate limit becomes exhausted and cries out for reversal' (Jullien, 1995: 194). On this view, tactics have a propensity to become strategy, but as soon as they do they harden, and at that point become liable to the very same reversals they had themselves enacted in their tactical modality. To explain this process, though, rather than simply describe it, we need to take a long view and try to see the whole.

See Figure 5.2 for how the square now looks.

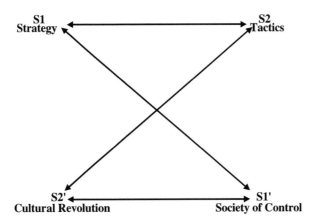

Figure 5.2

Now, we must decide what transcends the square as a whole, as well as what negates it. Only then will the properly dialectical nature of the picture we have drawn be revealed. In the first place, we would want to stipulate some kind of utopia, but that would seem to have already been proscribed by our earlier discussion of de Certeau's plane of immanence. And while I'm not about to have a sudden change of heart at this point, it does have to be acknowledged that there is more than one kind of utopia, and, what's more, some of them are of an explicitly religious cast. So while I have indeed argued that de Certeau's explicitly religious stance rules utopia out as a cardinal term in his discursive system, it is in fact utopia that functions here as the positive or transcendent term, only it is understood as a miraculous 'nowhere' not an inherent revolutionary process. And it is precisely de Certeau's deeply personalised account of the resistive power of belief as instanced in the popular Pernambuco legend of Frei Damião that directs us to this conclusion (1984: 15–16). By the same token, the same story points us toward history – understood as fatality – as the ultimate negative term, the one which would wipe clean the entire slate we have taken such pains to depict. In conclusion, then, let me rapidly enumerate why this should be so.

Using an imposed religion in an eccentric and eclectic fashion – for instance, they infuse it with superstition, the residual form in which practically deceased belief systems persist – the indigenous people of Pernambuco take stories like those of the miracles of Frei Damião and use them to counter the apparent fatality of their circumstances (de Certeau, 1984: 17–18). While it is true that the Pernambuco believed Frei Damião would somehow save them, it isn't as an indigenous form of messianism that de Certeau interprets this particular belief. Rather what de Certeau sees as important is the fact that story of the saint offers the people something else to believe in besides their present socio-economic plight and otherwise hopeless-looking political fate. This belief, as de Certeau explains, is utopian rather than deluded because it functions not to lull the mind and body with fables of golden futures to come, but rather to agitate the conscience with the surety that what is presently so is not *necessarily* so: 'It recognised in that injustice an order of things that seemed immutable: it is always so; people see it every day. But no legitimacy whatever was accorded this state of affairs. On the contrary, just because it was a constantly repeated fact, this relationship of forces did not become any more acceptable. The *fact* was not accepted as a *law*, even if it remained inescapably a fact' (de Certeau, 1984: 16). With the utopian possibility at the forefront of their thinking, the Pernambuco were free to *calculate* their future in contradiction to the facts.

In other words, no matter how powerful the colonising force was, because it didn't have any authority the people under its control remained free to believe otherwise than as instructed. This, according to de Certeau's (1997a) reckoning, is the basic nature of the transformation of French society enacted by the rioting students and workers of May 1968. The difference between the two examples, which is crucial to understanding de Certeau's overall position, is that the eclecticism of the Pernambuco is directed at the creation and perpetuation of an authority, something the people can believe in, while, at least in the saddened eyes of de Certeau himself, the trajectory of May 1968 lay in the opposite direction altogether, towards some kind despiritualised anarchy in which cynicism reigned supreme. The key message in de Certeau's retelling of the Frei Damião story, which I would argue defines the 'ethic' of de Certeau's project as a whole, is that the contradiction between the hopeful space of utopia and the hopeless one of the fatality of history must be produced and rendered as starkly as possible if one is not to give way to the other.[13] An eventuality that would result either in a dreamy world of simulacra and illusion such as those as imagined by futurologists as diverse as Baudrillard and Toffler, or the nightmare of the imprisoned soul that Foucault and before him Weber conjured. That is to say, one must work constantly to *produce the dialectic*. And this, I suggest, is what de Certeau has in mind when he speaks of preferring a cruel lucidity. Tactics are not libratory in the material sense of the word: the little victories of everyday life do no more (but, also, no less) than disrupt the fatality of the established order.

So, finally, the completed square looks like this.

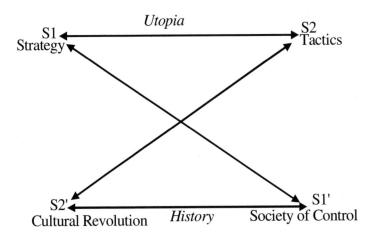

Figure 5.3

This is not the end of the story, however, but the point at which the real work can begin.

Notes

[1] Better examples of fleshed-out concepts include Foucault's (1979) 'discipline', Detienne and Vernant's (1978) 'metis' and Jullien's (1995) 'propensity'.

[2] For a detailed survey of the intellectual context of de Certeau's work in France at this time, see Rigby, 1991: 12–38.

[3] On this score, though, I would want to single out Alan Read's extraordinarily productive use of de Certeau – for both theatre criticism and practice in his *Theatre and Everyday Life* – as a genuine attempt to see the greater political implications of the little victories of the everyday. For an excellent critique of Fiske's too simplistic deployment of de Certeau, see Barcan, 1995: 89–92.

[4] For instance, both Fiske (1988) and Jenkins (1992) make far too much of *la perruque*, while Ross (1997) makes far too little of it. However, for more sober uses of this concept, see Ruddick (1990) and Yúdice (1988).

[5] I take as my signal 'proof' of this, de Certeau's repeated unwillingness to decide, finally, between any of the many possible models for cultural analysis he enumerates. An exemplary instance of this, which is by no means an isolated example (but on the contrary, an all too familiar one), is de Certeau's failure to decide which of the two counter models of reading he puts up against Lévi-Strauss he is going to opt for. Instead, he treats the different models as variants on a deeper, one assumes noumenal form (de Certeau, 1984: 175).

[6] The eradication in the Nouvelle Édition of *L'Invention du quotidien* (de Certeau, 1990) of a number of footnotes alluding to future undertakings now alas never to be completed are a mistake, I believe, because it fosters a sense of finality contrary to the spirit (and the actuality) of the work.

[7] 'The purpose of this work is to make explicit the systems of operational combination (*les combinatoires d'opérations*) which also compose a "culture", and to bring to light the models of action characteristic of users whose status as the dominated element in society (a status that does not mean they are either passive or docile) is concealed by the euphemistic term "consumers"' (de Certeau, 1984: xi–xii).

[8] Although it is obviously inspired by the work that culminated in the publication of *Anti-Oedipus* (Foucault [1979: 309] says as much), it differs from Deleuze and Guattari's project in this one respect: it does not offer an elaborate enough counter-system of lines of flight (Deleuze and Guattari [1987: 531] make this point themselves).

[9] 'Simplifying to the extreme, I define *postmodern* as incredulity toward metanarratives' (Lyotard, 1984: xxiv).

[10] For a critique of the application of the label 'practices' to everyday behaviours, see Ross, 1997.

[11] 'We're definitely moving toward "control societies" that are no longer exactly disciplinary. Foucault's often taken as the theorist of disciplinary societies and of their principle technology, *confinement* (not just in hospitals and prison, but in schools, factories, and barracks). But he was actually one of the first to say that we're moving away from disciplinary societies, we've already left them behind. We're moving toward control societies that no longer operate by confining people but through continuous control and instant communication' (Deleuze, 1995: 174).

[12] The 'function of any cultural revolution (such as must have accompanied all the great transitions from one mode of production to another) will be to invent the life habits of the new social world, to *de-program* subjects trained in the older one' (Jameson, 1992a: 164). The invention of new habits can be inaugurated by the dominant social order, as Jameson's account of postmodernism strongly suggests (that is, the idea that postmodern space calls on us to develop new habits, grow new organs of perception, and so on), so it should not be assumed that cultural revolutions are implicitly revolutionary in the 'good sense'. Rather, what they describe is the coming into view of social and cultural antagonisms and the indication of their possible resolutions (Jameson, 1991: 38–45).

[13] As such, I would argue that Clayton is off-beam in saying that de Certeau's conception of power is 'too optimistic' (1993: 23). If anything, as I have suggested, it is too pessimistic.

6. Unknotting Place and Space

It is within the possibilities of late capitalism that people glimpse the 'main chance', 'go for it', make money, and reorganise firms in new ways (just like artists or generals, ideologists or gallery owners).

Fredric Jameson, *Postmodernism, or, The Cultural Logic of Late Capitalism*

The contradiction adduced at the close of the previous chapter between the hopeful space of utopia and the hopeless one of the fatality of history frames de Certeau's theorisation of spatiality. However, this frame is itself further delimited by its own convulsive contradiction, which by taking Foucault's disciplinary society (together with some kind of opposing force of anti-discipline) as a given can be said to exist 'between the collective mode of administration and an individual mode of reappropriation' (de Certeau, 1984: 96). What this amounts to saying, is that, as the Marxian dictum has it: people make history, but not in conditions of their own choosing (de Certeau's well-worn slogan 'making do', really means nothing more controversial than this). This is the new scene for our inquiry into the actual work of strategy and tactics, which we know is spatial, without yet knowing anything about its peculiar mechanism.

In what follows I will limit myself to an explanation of this mechanism – what I offer here is an account of de Certeau's notion of spatiality, not an exegesis of its permutations 'place' and 'space'. As we shall see, this mechanism hails from psychoanalysis, but one has to do quite a bit of digging in order to see its working parts. Nowhere have I been able to find an account of de Certeau's theorisation of these terms connecting them to psychoanalysis.[1] Yet, as I will show here, not to do so is to fail to understand them altogether.

One of the difficulties I have with de Certeau's work is his reluctance to be singular about anything. He is compulsively pluralist in his approach. Often he flirts with a theory for a few pages, then quietly and politely dismisses it, but never in such an absolute way as to permit you to think he had negated it. On the contrary, he leaves you thinking that the idea touched upon so tantalisingly is going to return later in some more definitive fashion which would make this initial foray meaningful.

Usually though, no such return is made. Thus in thinking about de Certeau's theorisation of space one has to sort through a number of false starts, three of which are substantial enough to warrant being called 'false trails'. And it is only after one has worked through these three that one happens upon the 'true' path. The false trails are: (1) his consideration of Lefebvre, which is confined to a single, but momentous footnote (1984: 205n5); (2) his longer meditation on the intersection of pragmatics (Wittgenstein), linguistics (Benveniste) and speech act theory (Austin) which gives rise to the tempting analogy that rhetoric as a codified practice of using language might be used to analyse spatial practices (1984: 97–108); (3) his musing on Merleau-Ponty and his analytic distinction between 'geometric space' and 'anthropological space' (1984: 117–18). The 'true' path, or fourth trail appears like a sudden forking of the road in an amazing couple of lines linking his thoughts on space to Lacan's theory of the mirror stage (1984: 110).[2] The first three paths ultimately lead us nowhere insofar as de Certeau's conception of spatiality is concerned because de Certeau himself does not pursue them very far at all; it is only the last one, the connection to Lacan, that he doesn't simply mark out its existence (like some half-hearted trailblazer) and then move on. Although, having said that, neither does he explore it very much either.

Tom Conley's assertion that Lacan is an avowed master of de Certeau's (1988: xxivn7) will here take on the character of an imperative because it is only through the excavation of some of those now rather dusty and all but lost connections between Lacan and de Certeau that the latter's conceptual schema can be brought fully to light. It should be read as instructive, I believe, that even after carefully delineating the importance and usefulness of Merleau-Ponty's phenomenological conception of spatial existence – which gives rise to its own two quite useful analytic categories ('geometric space' and 'anthropological space') which I have discussed elsewhere (Buchanan, 1996b) but now find myself needing to place under erasure – de Certeau nevertheless opts for a different tact altogether: place and space, he says, will refer not to Merleau-Ponty's 'geometric space' and 'anthropological space' but rather to two sorts of determinations in stories. Meanwhile, stories themselves are to be seen as a kind of labour 'that constantly transforms places into spaces or spaces into places' (de Certeau, 1984: 118). Stories, though, are only the inner spring, as it were, of de Certeau's conception of space, not the thing itself.[3] A declaration like the one above must first be treated as a problem: what kind of theory of space can incorporate stories in this way?

It is at this point that we need to dig beneath the surface and start looking for a Lacanian scheme, for I read de Certeau's uptake of Lacan over Merleau-Ponty as an attempt to get past the purely perceptual to some more epistemological conception of space.[4] Its seductive quest-narrative 'feeling tone', which I will point up in what follows, should thus be central to our understanding of it. However, while it is true de Certeau sets aside Merleau-Ponty's phenomenological conception of space, he does not, for all that, reject it out of hand. Like Lacan himself, de Certeau seems to accept Merleau-Ponty's phenomenological conception of space as an adequate account of the 'given' of spatiality all while wanting something more from it that phenomenology cannot give without betraying its own taboo on metaphysics. What both Lacan and de Certeau want in addition to phenomenology's strictly rationalist account of the cognitive apprehension of space is an irrational – paranoid or schizoid – dimension which can take into account those uses of space, such as sacralisation, that fall outside the boundaries of reason.[5] From this point of view, taking Merleau-Ponty's work as the measure of the spatial given in de Certeau, but bearing in mind he wants to move beyond this point, there is much to be gained, I believe, by re-making their acquaintance. So, I will try to show how de Certeau relies on Merleau-Ponty but eventually places him under erasure in favour of Lacan.

Looking down on Manhattan from the 110th floor of the World Trade Centre de Certeau was struck by the fact that from there he could 'see the whole' of New York. From this dizzying vantage point the entire city was spread out before him like a map – if he wanted to he could read it like a map. 'To be lifted to the summit of the World Trade Centre is to be lifted out of the city's grasp. One's body is no longer clasped by the streets that turn and return it according to an anonymous law; nor is it possessed, whether as player or played, by the rumble of so many differences and by the nervousness of New York traffic' (de Certeau, 1984: 92). But, he wonders, is one really seeing New York? Can the city really be seen in this way? What is it to really see? 'Must one finally fall back into the dark space where crowds move back and forth, crowds that, though visible from on high, are themselves unable to see down below?' (de Certeau, 1984: 92). What de Certeau finds here is a parable for the problem to theory represented by the practice of reading. 'The 1370 foot high tower that serves as a prow for Manhattan continues to construct the fiction that creates readers, makes the complexity of the city readable, and immobilises its opaque mobility in a transparent text' (de Certeau, 1984: 92).

The problem, de Certeau finds, is that the life of the city, the constellation of lives that make a city what it is, the actual experience of the city, in other words, is not contained in the concept of the city. Lives cannot be mapped in this way – cannot be read – or even truly rendered readable by maps (though of course it is only through maps that they can be read): something always slips away.[6] Merleau-Ponty shows that de Certeau's concern with respect to an ethnography formulated on the basis of such a view of the city is philosophically well-founded.

Perception itself, Merleau-Ponty argues, is impossible from so isolated, and, given its God-like pretensions, ironically relativist position. 'When I walk around my flat, the various aspects in which it presents itself to me could not possibly appear as views of one and the same thing if I did not know that each of them represents the flat seen from one spot or another, and if I were unaware of my movements, and of my body as retaining its identity through the stages of those movements' (Merleau-Ponty, 1962: 203). It is the memory of who one is and where one has been that enables any kind of a view to be put together. Here then, under the auspices of memory, Merleau-Ponty's crucial philosophical move, which de Certeau's theorisation of space implicitly endorses, is to posit the body (as the bearer of memory) as the necessary condition of perception.

Theoretically, a (mental) bird's eye view is always possible; one can always visualise a city as flattened and thus draw a plan of it.[7] But even then, Merleau-Ponty argues, one 'could not grasp the unity of the object without the mediation of bodily experience' (1962: 203). What we call a plan is, after all, only 'a more comprehensive perspective' (Merleau-Ponty, 1962: 203) and in order to have that more comprehensive perspective an embodied subject that 'can view successively *from* various positions' (Merleau-Ponty, 1962: 203) is required. The city can be seen from above and comprehended as a living map only because it can also be seen from below, from in amongst the traffic. Merleau-Ponty thus proposed that a distinction – which will be crucial to de Certeau's rethinking of spatiality, even if it only operates in ghostly form – be made between 'geometric space'[8] and 'anthropological space' (de Certeau, 1984: 93; 117). This distinction manifests itself in de Certeau's work in the polemical contrast he draws between the 'urban *fact*' (1984: 94) (anthropological) and the '*concept* of a city' (1984: 94) (geometric). On the one hand then, there is the concept of the city which 'like a proper name' (de Certeau, 1984: 94) enables an unstable and boundless mass to be managed, comprehended even, and on the other there is the experience of the city which is transitory and has 'no readable identity' (de Certeau, 1984: 95). The concept city is an administrative gesture akin to Said's (1991) notion of Orientalism inasmuch as it makes the city manageable. Meanwhile, the experience of the city, like the people described as Orientals – but who do not identify with that label as such (except in that subversive mimicking way Bhabha [1995] describes) – is actually 'impossible to administer' (de Certeau, 1984: 95).

Later, wandering those same city streets, the teeming 'down there' he witnessed from atop the World Trade Centre, de Certeau wonders how might the city be conceived *if not* from a God's perspective (1984: 97). According to Merleau-Ponty, if we insist on the uniformity of space, and refuse to acknowledge the inherent diversity of perspectives intersubjectivity entails we cannot help but *be* God-like (1962: 255). It is precisely this eventuality and its accompanying feeling of inevitably that de Certeau senses he must counter, yet do so without imposing still another rigid scheme (hence his ambiguous usage of Lacan, I will suggest). As de Certeau put it (citing Merleau-Ponty), the problem is that: "'there are as many spaces as there are distinct spatial experiences'"(1984: 118). His solution is to engage with 'ways of being', or stories as he chose to call them, rather than 'states of being' and so rewrite spatiality in terms of perspective to give it a more thoroughly active voice. This is, of course, precisely what strategy and tactics codify. The logical extension of this approach, insofar as an analysis of a cultural milieu is concerned, is to focus on 'ways of seeing' rather than 'what is seen'.

Merleau-Ponty does not allow perception to be abstracted from either the perceiving subject or the perceived object; on the contrary, it is the process of perception itself which enables these critical items, a perceiving subject, and a perceived object, to be isolated. To perceive is, at the same time, to be for the object, and to be for the subject – perception brings the subject and object as discrete entities into existence, it gives them an intellectual liveliness and significance, but it does not confer upon them an ontological status. It could not, since neither item is conceivable outside of the process of perception itself. Just as importantly, the distinction itself would not be possible outside of a notion of spatiality. Space is what allows the relation of perceiving to perceived to be formulated, it is the distance between subject and object that enables them to be distinguished from each other by perception. But, it also conserves the indistinction precisely by being what must be between subject and object. Thus space is 'in' perception, at the same time as it is what is perceived by perception. Such that whatever perceives must perceive itself as it is perceiving others.

In parenthesis, I think it is worth pointing out that de Certeau is not – by focusing on spatialising – attempting to romanticise the pedestrian, or reconceive commuting by foot across the city as a revolutionary act. Benjamin's *flâneurs* are for this reason inconsistent with the archetypical characters de Certeau refers to, the nameless *Wandersmanner* (1992: 14), as each would be just one possible type of city-user among countless others, and should not be accorded any special privilege for a theory of space.[9] This is not to say, though, that Benjamin's analysis of the city is without interest.[10] His insistence on the importance of memory is especially pertinent. However, it has become something of a reflex to compare Benjamin's discussion of *flânerie* in Second Empire Paris as it is evoked by Baudelaire's prose and poetry to de Certeau's attempt to capture the purposive purposeless of pedestrians in latter day New York (Bruno, 1993: 162; Donald, 1992: 437). Yet, apart from the fact that more than a century separates Benjamin's Capital of the Nineteenth-Century from de Certeau's Big

Apple, and that such spatio-temporal alterity cannot be so simply glossed as it must be to compare the two, it should also be obvious that what Benjamin describes is a peculiar type of city-user, whereas what de Certeau has in view is the most ordinary of city-users. Although by disposition he is a 'man of the crowd', because of his special qualities the *flâneur* is actually a man apart from the crowd. In contrast, the person de Certeau has in mind is entirely without qualities and therefore indistinguishable from the crowd. The eclipse of this crucial difference between Benjamin's historical project and de Certeau's quasi-ethnographic project has led to some rather unfortunate romanticizations of de Certeau's theory of space.[11] As such, I tend to agree with Read (1993: 162–7), who seems to suggest that the better link between de Certeau and Benjamin, if one needs be made, is Benjamin's 'storyteller' rather than his *flâneur*.

At length, then, having read into the record that which de Certeau accepts but consciously quarantines, we must now turn to the equally buried but unconsciously suppressed Lacanian connection. All spatial practice, de Certeau asserts, must be seen as a repetition – direct or indirect – of that primordial advent to spatiality, as we might now want to call it, namely 'the child's differentiation from the mother's body. It is through that experience that the possibility of space and of a localisation (a "not everything") of the subject is inaugurated' (1984: 109). No matter how well it is accepted that *The Practice of Everyday Life* is an experimental, which is to say suggestive, not conclusive, kind of work, nothing prepares you for the shock of this connection between spatial practices and psychoanalysis, around which, as you only too groggily gather, the whole of his theorisation of space will ultimately revolve (which is to say, *not* speech act theory as one is initially led to suppose); nor, I might add, does he offer anything to follow it that might alleviate that shock. The clincher here is the disturbing fact that de Certeau's long meditation on the interesting possibility of a 'walking rhetorics' uses the analogy it draws between pedestrian practices and speech acts to conclude that both, at some ultimate level we cannot really reach except by abstraction, are oneiric. 'From this point of view, after having compared pedestrian processes to linguistic formations, we can bring them back down in the direction of oneiric figuration, or at least discover on that other side what, in spatial practice, is inseparable from the dreamed place' (de Certeau 1984: 103). It is clear from this that de Certeau always intended to take his meditations on space in a Lacanian direction, but he had first of all to manufacture a vocabulary for himself which he did by appropriating rhetoric.

From here we move directly into a psychoanalytic figuring of spatiality via the following aphorism: 'To walk is to lack a place. It is the indefinite process of being absent and in search of a proper' (de Certeau 1984: 103). Although we now understand that lack should be interpreted in a Lacanian manner, there is, however, no new theorisation of the relationship between dreams and spaces to speak of, only the bald assertion of it and a few sketchy suggestions as to how it might be made to apply analytically. Nor, I must add, is there any discussion of how the analysis is going to overcome its own altogether regressive emphasis on the imaginary: the mirror stage, as is well known, precipitates the advent into the symbolic order, at which point it is reorganised along new lines; the imago of the father takes on the character of the Law and so on. As such, the truly interesting question one wants to ask of this uptake of a Lacanian notion of spatiality is how is the shift to the Symbolic Order going to be accommodated at ground level? Basically, though, we are simply left to ponder de Certeau's uptake of Lacan like those koans with which Lacan himself was so fond of bewildering his audiences (it is timely, perhaps, to recall that de Certeau was an assiduous frequenter of those smoky, hospital-basement gatherings).

In order to make any sense of it, then, we have to backtrack a couple of steps and try to fathom just what hermeneutic possibilities de Certeau had in mind in speaking so allusively. The point of any koan being, I take it, to force us to imagine the conditions in which it would not be senseless. First, then, let me spell out the koan in full. De Certeau envisions spatial practices, which in themselves stand in greater need of definition than is originally supplied but can be taken to mean more or less anything that involves movement (including the movement of thought itself), as re-enactments of what Lacan called the 'mirror stage': 'In the initiatory game, just as in the "joyful activity" of the child who, standing before a mirror, sees itself as *one* (it is *she* or *he*, seen as a whole) but *another* (*that*, an image with which the child identifies itself), what counts is the process of this "spatial captation" that inscribes the passage towards the other as the law of being and the law of place. To practice place is thus to repeat the joyful and silent experience of childhood; it is, in a place, *to be other and to move toward the other*' (de Certeau, 1984: 109–10).

It is obviously this last phrase, which de Certeau himself took the trouble to emphasise, that provides the crucial map coordinates we need to find the buried treasure, namely Lacan's L-Schema. But before coming to that it may be helpful if we take one further step back and look at the original case study, which is rapidly becoming a 'primal scene' in its own right, something which needs to be averted at all costs. Although de Certeau explicitly states that we do not have to go back to the infamous analysis Freud made of his eighteen month old grandson's wooden-reel game in order to understand his point (1984: 109), in practice we do if we want to get the full picture. By the same token, a brief return to Freud will permit us to flesh out the hermeneutic model de Certeau seems to have in mind, but doesn't ultimately provide sufficient detail for it to be of much use to us. This means, of course, that much of what follows is bound to be speculative, both in respect of its own content and in its relation to de Certeau's thought. I'm afraid, though, that I don't see that there is much choice: either one dismisses de Certeau's speculations on space as incomplete and therefore incoherent, or one endeavours to use what is there in order to go forward and make something of them. To that end, I will use Freud as my starting point, but after working through that (as well as Lacan's subsequent mediations) I will square the circle so to speak with Jameson.

As is surely legend by now, Lacan takes his notion of the mirror stage from a brief footnote – evidently something of an afterthought on Freud's part – in that section of *Beyond the Pleasure Principle* where Freud recounts his grandson's so-called 'fort/da' game. Initially the grandson's game simply consisted in him tossing any small object to hand as far away as his little arms could manage. Success in this matter was accompanied by a satisfied and drawn-out 'o-o-o-o' sound by the child, which both his mother and grandfather interpreted as a nascent (that is, not yet properly phoneticised) 'fort', the German word for gone. At first Freud thought this was all there was to it, but he learned there was in fact two parts to the game. However, it wasn't until the child got a hold of a wooden-reel with string tied to it that he found the technical means to enact the second part of the game: 'What he did was to hold the reel by the string and very skilfully throw it over the edge of his curtained cot, so that it disappeared into it, at the same time uttering his expressive "o-o-o-o". He then pulled the reel out of the cot again by the string and hailed its reappearance with a joyful "*da*" ["there"]. This, then, was the complete game – disappearance and return. As a rule one only witnessed its first act, which was repeated untiringly as a game in itself, though there is no doubt that the greater pleasure was attached to the second act' (Freud, 1984: 284). Confirmation of this last point concerning the greater yield of pleasure, which is the one I want to examine here, comes in the form of the footnote already mentioned.

> One day the child's mother had been away for several hours and on her return was met with the words 'Baby o-o-o-o!' which was at first incomprehensible. It soon turned out, however, that during this long period of solitude the child had found a method of making *himself* disappear. He had discovered his reflection in a full-length mirror which did not quite reach to the ground, so that by crouching down he could make his mirror-image 'gone'. (Freud, 1984: 284n1)

Freud interprets the game in terms of the achievement of a necessary instinctual renunciation – the game, as Freud saw it, was in fact a compensatory device or mechanism by which the child re-staged the otherwise intolerable disappearance of his mother in such a way as to render it bearable. While he couldn't prevent his mother from leaving him, he could orchestrate the disappearance of any object to hand and this, thanks to its cathartic value, provided the hapless child with the means of bearing the inward-pressure the renunciation of his instincts placed on him. But since the child cannot have taken any joy from his mother's departure, repeating that departure over and over again via a re-staging of it in a game would seem, at best, masochistic. Yet that is not at all the conclusion Freud draws; indeed, it is precisely against that impression of child play that he offers this example. Freud's question is, then, what is the source of the pleasure of this game? Freud suggests there are two ways in which the child yields pleasure from his rehearsing of this manifestly unpleasurable scenario of the uncontrolled leave-taking of his mother: first of all, responding perhaps to an instinct for mastery which has no bearing on the content of the situation as such, but refers rather to the intolerable form of the situation, the child uses the game to transform his passive state into an active one – play, on this view, becomes an instrument of transformation; by the same token, and this is the second source of pleasure, it may just be that the child is using the game as a way of displacing his anger and is simply revenging himself on his mother by tossing the toy (her) aside. This latter interpretation is not of course incompatible with the former, a fact which Lacan plays upon.

Lacan's treatment of this scenario differs from Freud's in precisely the area of the yield of pleasure: for Lacan it is the joyful repetition of the activity that stands in most need of explanation, it is that which must be underwritten with a very particular type of pleasure. Unable to talk, walk, nor properly even stand upright without some kind of support – mechanical or parental – the child at this decisive age, still under eighteen months, is in fact outstripped by a chimpanzee of the same age in the area of instrumental intelligence, yet he or she is capable of something the primate cannot manage: he or she can recognise themselves in a mirror. That it is in fact recognition, a necessary prelude to identification, that is at stake here is confirmed, Lacan suggests, by the child's incessant 'play' with this newly discovered image – this newly discovered production of self we should also say. From an ethological point of view, 'it is an expression of situational apperception, an essential stage of the act of intelligence' (Lacan, 1977: 1). From a psychoanalytic point of view, it is *the* instant of spatial captation; *the* moment, in other words, when the child is suddenly able to formulate a clear and workable distinction between their own body, understood but vaguely at this point as a discontinuous series of organs, or little machines, amounting to a precious interiority that knows no exteriority, and their environment, of which they develop an increasingly complex picture as time passes by experimenting with it. This moment, in general, corresponds to what Lacan called the

Imaginary, which, it must be remembered, is always about to be superseded by the Symbolic.

The comparative immaturity of the child at this stage in its life, still stuck in the Imaginary, as it were, is crucial to Lacan's interpretation of this game of recognition, because he sees it as being essentially the pleasure one gets from anticipating what will become of one (for an adult, it is the pleasure one might take in contemplating life after study – one's degree on this view of things is the mirror in which we perceive that Other self we are ceaselessly moving towards while completing our studies without ever really knowing what it would entail to be that Other self). The child does not see themselves in the mirror, not their present fragmentary self at any rate – no one ever does see themselves in a mirror, of course, since it is only an *image* of oneself that appears there – but a future self, a *Gestalt* that does not suffer any of the infirmities of extreme youth, in short, an ideal self. Strictly speaking, then, as Lacan frequently emphasises, what the child really sees in the mirror can only be described as a misrecognition of self. Not so much an image as an imago, that is to say, not an image for passive contemplation but one for active assumption (or, in more familiar terms, identification); what the child sees in the mirror is a vision of what they can be, what all being well they believe they are going to be; as such, the imago is a kind of predestination, or article of faith. It is the 'I' given in its primordial form, 'before it is objectified in the dialectic of the identification with the other, and before language restores to it, in the universal, its function as subject' (Lacan, 1977: 2).

In the Imaginary phase, the child is unaware of the distinction that we know only too well exists between ourselves and others; in fact, until they see themselves in a mirror children do not even know they are a discrete entity distinct from either their mother or their physical environment. It is all of one to them at this point, before the imago takes a hold of their imaginary, which is why Lacan describes the transformative process inaugurated by the mirror stage as spatial captation. From this moment on, though, having seen their self *as* self for the first time, the child is no longer able to see the world except in terms of a proliferation of others and the thick, almost womb-like space of infancy gives way to a semiotically saturated space they will struggle for the rest of their lives to master. 'Indeed, for the *imagos* – whose veiled faces it is our privilege to see in outline in our daily experience and in the penumbra of symbolic efficacity – the mirror-image would seem to be the threshold of the visible world, if we go by the mirror disposition that the *imago of one's own body* presents in hallucinations or dreams' (Lacan, 1977: 3). In other words, the mirror stage establishes the relationship between the child and his or her environment by giving the child the technical means of making the distinction between the two. But in so doing for ever destroys the comfortable feeling of mastery they once knew.

At the same time, however, another kind of tension is brought into play, which Lacan describes as temporal: and this is the drama of primordial jealousy, which invariably manifests itself as aggressivity. Aggressivity, on the Lacanian view of things, is the correlative of the narcissistic mode of identification for which the mirror stage is the archetype. Narcissism is probably best thought of as the self-adoring end of a spectrum of behaviours that really begins with a wilfully ignorant and utterly arrogant belief that one is at the centre of all things, that literally there are no others. Recognition of the mirror image as oneself is thus in the first instance a cancelling out of others and a preservation of a certain primordiality, albeit at the price of its alienation. This relationship between the emerging ego and its mirror-image Other is ultimately erotic: the child invests his or her libidinal energy via this image, which is why desire for Lacan is always the desire of the Other (hence, too, the zigzag map of the path of desire we know as the L-Schema). It is this investment which in the end will give rise to the fully-armoured form of the ego itself. This form crystallises in the tumult of the subject's inner conflicts determining the very arousal of his or her desire for the object of the other's desire. But, what Lacan calls 'the primordial coming together' (1977: 19), or *concours*, of the ego and its Other, is, in the very moment of its erotic self-identification, in fact precipitated into an indistinct 'aggressive competitiveness' (1977: 19), or *concurrence*, out of which there develops the basic Lacanian triad of others, the ego and the object. All of which, manifests itself as, and is confirmed by, a transitivism: 'The child who strikes another says that he has been struck; the child who sees another fall cries' (Lacan, 1977: 19).

> The Imaginary may thus be described as a peculiar spatial configuration, whose bodies primarily entertain relationships of inside/outside with one another, which is then traversed and reorganised by that primordial rivalry and transitivisitic substitution of imagoes, that indistinction of primary narcissism and aggressivity, from which our later conceptions of good and evil derive. This stage is already an alienation – the subject having been captivated by his or her specular image – but in Hegelian fashion it is the kind of alienation from which a more positive evolution is indistinguishable and without which the latter is inconceivable. The same must be said for the next stage of psychic development, in which the Imaginary itself is assumed into the Symbolic Order by way of its alienation by language. (Jameson, 1988a: 87)

The mirror stage establishes the relationship between us and the environment, which for all intents and purposes is what 'space' actually names. Space, then, as it emerges here is a complex term mapping a manifold relationship between two equally complicated terms. The better the picture we are able to obtain of these constituent notions – the subject and the environment – the better our understanding of space will be. This is why I began with an account of the deep background work of Merleau-Ponty. By the same token, though, we cannot overlook the fact that what space names is a relationship. Now, as we've seen, the mirror stage brokers this relationship in the first instance, but it is only one stage in a long sequence of events and transformations that eventually leads to the full maturation of the subject *as* subject and although we have been taught by Freud (via his important rejection of the image of modern Rome built on the ruins of ancient Rome as an adequate expression of the relation between the conscious and unconscious) to apprehend these stages synchronically, one nevertheless has to take account of them as transitions. The mirror stage, as we now know, is the advent of the child into the symbolic, which even if it carries with it a distant memory of wordless infancy cannot be reversed. Once alienated by language there is no going back. And this, it seems to me, is a point which de Certeau fatally fails to stress.

The mirror stage performs as its essential work the creation of the conditions for the child's access to the Symbolic Order: it does this by initiating a primordial form of alienation that is extended more or less infinitely throughout adult life by a play of substitutions. The fact we can be captivated by one imago, namely ourselves as Other, means we can by captivated by any number of other Imagoes providing the proper mediation can be engineered for the occasion. Ultimately, this is fate of all desire, in the Lacanian system: *to be other and to move toward the other*. This, in short, is the L-Schema, 'in which the subject's conscious desire, which she understands as a relationship between the desired object (*a*) and her ego or her self (*a'*), is mediated by the more fundamental relationship between the real subject (*S*) and the capital *A* of the Other [*Autre*], language, or the unconscious' (Jameson, 1988a: 93). The connection that, in a moment, I will want to make between de Certeau and Jameson is to be coordinated by precisely this rather remarkable mechanism, whose spatial extension is elaborated by Lacan in the following way:

> Let us say that animal psychology has shown us that the individual's relation to a particular field is, in certain species, mapped socially, in a way that raises it to the category of subjective membership. I would say that it is the subjective possibility of the mirror projection of such a field into the field of the other that gives human space its originally 'geometrical' structure, a structure that I would be happy to call *kaleidoscopic*. (Lacan, 1977: 27)

The social totality is the city, I will argue. And it is precisely the difficulty de Certeau has – in his justly famous chapter on pedestrianism – in finding an acceptable means of articulating the city *as* totality, and the celebrated way in which he worries over the various attempts he does permit himself to make, neither the precision of the map nor the hugger-mugger of the crowd proving adequate, in the end, that leads me to this conclusion. The whole fable of the visit to the World Trade Centre can be read as a search for a mirror in which to see a *Gestalt* of a kind sufficiently compelling to enable him to put the everyday into perspective; his failure to find such a mirror is then the point of the story. On such a quest, a pluralist can only redeem himself by failing to totalise. De Certeau's practice – at times infuriating – of trialling several different conceptual schemes alongside one another without indicating a strong preference for any of them, exhibited nowhere more insistently than in his many discussions of space, has the feel not so much of a modernist bricolage as a postmodern refusal to totalise. That it results in a conceptually – if not politically – weak pluralism is in fact deliberate, or at any rate purposive. One cannot denounce totalisation by replacing one strong totality with another, which of course explains why Lacan's L-schema is so obscure in de Certeau's work.

However tempted de Certeau might have been by its explanatory force, he has to repress the actual schema itself because the L-schema is an example par excellence of heterological reasoning, which we know he is more than a little suspicious of (to say the least). The problem, here, though is that if one doesn't follow Lacan, then one is stuck with Freud's rather too inconclusive 'story'. My feeling is that de Certeau's discussion of spatial stories is caught between this aconceptual moment in Freud and what one gathers is a too conceptual moment in the successor's work and is in that sense incompletely theorised. This can of course be rewritten in terms of orientation, the one towards the past (a return to the womb, the anxiety of childbirth and so on in Freud), and the other towards the future (the anticipation of a functional wholeness in Lacan). Read in these terms one can more readily see why being stuck in limbo between the two should strike me as so fraught. Indeed, this goes a long way towards explaining what I find so problematic in the work of Marc Augé, whose theorisation of space owes much to de Certeau's and can, in this respect, stand as the monitory example prompting us to pick up the Lacanian thread. For Augé, the future has been blanked out by capitalism, not fragmented as such, which is the story postmodernism generally tells, but emptied, rendered generic and soulless, which leaves only the past as a source of plenitude. Unable to anticipate new spaces, Augé is more or less compelled to long for those old spaces that had the richness of character the new ones lack (Augé 1995; 1998; and for my critique of Augé: Buchanan, 1999).

Now, having emphasised de Certeau's sins of omission more than enough, I want to attempt something of a valorisation of what is there by engineering something of a return of the repressed. For it seems to me that de Certeau does in fact offer something original and interesting in his conception of space, but it takes some getting to. By which I mean, it only stands out in relief. What I aim to show is that read alongside Jameson, de Certeau's notion of space suggests an interesting modification of the latter's 'cognitive mapping'.[12] This is the moment then to attempt to square the circle, as it were, if such a confused geometrical figure can be still made to apply, and make good on the promise of a sturdier connection between de Certeau and Jameson. I read de Certeau's fable of the visit to the World Trade Centre in New York city as an analogue to Jameson's rationale for dispensing with the initially promising notion of the cognitive map. Both accounts respond to what I have stressed throughout is the deeper problem of cultural studies: namely, the problem of representation. In de Certeau's case, as I've already argued with respect to several other conceptual models and schemes that de Certeau finds himself rejecting, the problem with the map is that it is simply not up to the job of representing the everyday in its full vivacity. While for Jameson the technology of the map has been superseded by the world-system itself, which has become far more complicated than the one maps were originally made to apply. Jameson reports on the failure of his own concept as follows:

> A new sense of global social structure was supposed to take on figuration and to displace the purely perceptual substitute of the geographical figure; cognitive mapping, which was meant to have a kind of oxymoronic value and to transcend the limits of mapping altogether, is, as a concept, drawn back by the force of gravity of the black hole of the map itself (one of the most powerful of all human conceptual instruments) and therein cancels out its own impossible originality. (Jameson, 1991: 416)

The reason I want to make this connection between de Certeau and Jameson, which may ultimately appear a little forced, though I hope to show they are cognate, is that I think Jameson offers the means of solving the problem of articulating the transition from the Imaginary to the Symbolic which de Certeau glosses but does not theorise. I can agree with de Certeau's hypothesis that all spatial practice is a repetition of the mirror stage, but only by instituting Jameson's notion of the cognitive map in the place of his supposed but unspecified mirror. The cognitive map, as Jameson explains it in *The Geopolitical Aesthetic*, is the picture we have of ourselves in the midst of the world-system: it is at once the attempt to grasp some larger totality that we desperately want to think of as the whole, though secretly fear isn't, and the determination of one's place in that totality. Interestingly enough, Jameson's uptake of the notion of a cognitive map follows a similar path to de Certeau's embracing of Lacan in that it is also preceded by a certain setting aside of a phenomenological given, in this case Kevin Lynch rather than Merleau-Ponty (such a move is of course entirely predictable given Jameson's allegiance to Sartre). Although Jameson graciously states that he takes the concept itself from Lynch (1991: 51), nowhere does Lynch (1960) in fact use the term 'cognitive map' himself – his own term is 'image' and rather than speaking of mapping he speaks of something he chooses to call 'imageability'. The main difference, however, is that for Lynch it is purely a matter of city design itself that determines whether a city can be grasped cognitively or not, whereas for Jameson the constitution of the subject is at least as crucial a factor. In fact, more precisely, it is the growing schism or lag between the two, the city outpacing the subject, that is the cause of those problems Jameson identifies as symptoms of postmodernity (1991: 44).

The cognitive map is that which we feel we need in order to locate ourselves in the contemporary world, and it may well be underpinned by a certain nostalgia for the simplicity of the mirror stage when to locate oneself one simply heaved oneself upright in front a mirror and lo and behold 'there one is!' Suggesting that it is indeed motivated, at least partly, by nostalgia, is the fact that such a scene is replayed endlessly in contemporary film: that redemptive moment of self discovery, when the hero, but more usually the heroine, finally takes account of their situation and faces up to themself, almost always occurs in front of the mirror. In a recent spate of films, *Great Expectations*, *As Good as it Gets* and *Titanic*, this perhaps too obvious device has been modified slightly and given the form of a portrait painting, allowing a closer correlation to be made between the heroine's becoming a subject and being a love object. Doubtless this is because long after it has ceased to function as an agent of captation the mirror continues to function as an effective symbol of it. But one could also read it, following Jameson's deployment of Sartre (1991: 44), as an analogon: by showing that it is always possible to reckon one's place in the world simply by taking a good hard look in the mirror what such scenes do is mediate between us as subjects and the world-system itself as Other. They give us the means and the courage to make the connection between ourselves as purely local entities and the world-system as a properly global one. By the same token, the frequent recourse (compulsion to repeat) to so unimaginative a device as the mirror itself may be read as a sign of a rising fear of a system wide failure to think locatability at all in postmodernity: it is the symbolic equivalent of that last stage of regression in which one is still sane but only barely before complete catatonia sets in and one freefalls into autism (the great narrative of this process is of course Günter Grass's *The Tin Drum*).

Now, as I suggested earlier, the really interesting question one wants answered by de Certeau is just how in his retelling of the mirror stage is the Imaginary going to brought under the yoke of the Symbolic. Without ever stipulating that it is this question he is answering, though it seems safe to assume that it is, de Certeau suggests there are two main ways in which the anticipatory *gestalt* of that originary moment is rendered concrete. These in fact are the two main 'practices' he suggests we use we locate ourselves in everyday life: (1) the attribution place names (de Certeau, 1984: 103) and (2) the telling of stories about those places (de Certeau, 1984: 121). 'In the spaces brutally lit by an alien reason, proper names carve out pockets of hidden and familiar meanings. They "make sense"; in other words, they are the impetus of movements, like vocations and calls that turn or divert an itinerary by giving it a meaning (or a direction) (*sens*) that was previously unforeseen. These names create a nowhere in places; they change them into passages' (de Certeau, 1984: 104). 'In a pre-established geography, which extends (if we limit ourselves to the home) from bedrooms so small that "one can't do anything in them" to the legendary, long-lost attic that "could be used for everything", everyday stories tell us what one can do in it and make out of it. They are treatments of space' (de Certeau, 1984: 122).[13] These practices convert the pure spatiality (I have limited myself to) into *place*. As it turns out, these are also the two mechanisms Jameson suggests play a crucial locational role in postmodern existence, though he rewrites them as (1) naming the system and (2) geopolitical aesthetics and makes them more explicitly problems of representation.

> Whether representation can draw directly, in some new way, on the distinctive technology capitalism's third stage, whose video- and computer-based furniture and object-world are markedly less photogenic than the media and transportation technology of the second (not excluding telephones), remains one of the great open questions of postmodern culture generally. Surely the newer spy novels, with their bewildering multiplication of secret or private espionage operations within public ones ... go a certain way towards declaring at least the intent to construct a narrative which is in some way an *analogon* of and a stand-in for the unimaginable overdetermination of the computer itself. But in representations like these, the operative effect is confusion rather than articulation. It is at the point where we give up and are no longer able to remember which side the characters are on, and how they have been revealed to be hooked up with the other ones, that we have presumably grasped the deeper truth of the world ... Such confusions – which evidently have something to do with structural limits of memory – seem to mark a point of no return beyond which the human organism can no longer match the velocities or the demographies of the new world-system. (Jameson, 1992b: 16)

For Jameson, and by extension for de Certeau, the twin practice of naming and storytelling is the primary means we have at our disposal at the present time for producing our cognitive maps. The juxtaposition of these two attempts at theorising spatial captation has the salutary effect of interpolating ideology, via misrecognition, into the heart of the cognitive map itself, something which neither Jameson nor de Certeau really allows for (though one assumes that Jameson at least would have no objection to such a move). The crucial difference between the two uses of this concept, is in how these two temperamentally opposite thinkers deal with their respective failure to produce a lasting and fully satisfying instance of such a map. As we know, both consider it a more or less forlorn hope that so complex a thing as the world-system could in fact be mapped, either because one cannot fit daily life into a concept without squeezing the life out of it first, or because it is beyond our imaginative capacity to grasp so huge a web of connections. But for the one, Jameson, the ongoing effort to grasp the totality, to name it and to picture it, is what counts; while for the other, de Certeau, naming and storytelling is what one is reduced to, what one does in order to make the uninhabitable immensity just that little bit more livable. Perhaps now it can be seen why I felt it necessary to begin by analysing de Certeau's relation to utopia: there is a kind of hopelessness here that colours everything, even that which might on first flush have seemed romantic and charming.

Notes

[1] Although Thrift (1996: 21) perceives de Certeau's obvious debt to Freud he does not make the connection between de Certeau and Lacan.

[2] On the first three of these knots, see Buchanan, 1994; 1995; 1996b; 1997.

[3] For an important, early analysis of the function of stories in de Certeau's overall conceptual schema see, Silverstone, 1989.

[4] Lacan's own commentary on the aims of his own project and its relation to Merleau-Ponty's can be found in Lacan, 1979: 71–6.

[5] From this perspective, David Harvey's pointing up of a certain sympathy between the respective spatial theories of Whitehead and de Certeau is, while exceedingly interesting, regressive: it takes us 'backwards' in the direction of the coolly rational, and not forwards in the direction of the metaphysical (1996: 261–3).

[6] 'The map, a totalizing stage on which elements of diverse origin are brought together to form tableau of a "state" of geographical knowledge, pushes away into its prehistory or into its posterity, as if into the wings, the operations of which it is the result or the necessary condition. It remains alone on the stage' (de Certeau, 1984: 121). The same problematic underpins Soja's *Postmodern Geographies*: 'Totalizing visions, attractive though they may be, can never capture all the meanings and significations of the urban when the landscape is critically read and envisioned as a fulsome geographical text' (1989: 247).

[7] Kevin Lynch's book *The Image of the City* (1960) takes as its research object the discovery of physical factors impeding this ability.

[8] Lacan too utilises a notion of geometric space. The geometral space of vision, Lacan says, 'is perfectly reconstructible, imaginable by a blind man

[sic]' (Lacan, 1979: 86). That is to say, the geometral as that which makes space thinkable is also a gesture of thought. It is the condition and object.

[9] Rosello's (1994) failure to make this crucial distinction between Benjamin's *flâneurs* and the *Wandersmanner* de Certeau mentions damages what, to my mind, is an otherwise exceedingly interesting deployment of the notion of *Wandersmanner* to discuss cyberspace and hypertext.

[10] But one would certainly want to agree with Jameson's assessment of it as both 'singularly relevant and singularly antiquated' (1991: 45).

[11] On this point, while I share Margaret Morse's concern (1990: 195) that anachronistic concepts of space and spatiality taken from the nineteenth century (such as Baudelaire's) should not be used to account for twentieth-century spaces (such as freeways and malls) I do not agree that de Certeau's concepts are so derived. His main writing on space was produced while living in the USA and far from being 'premall' and 'prefreeway' it is geared to understanding precisely those kinds of structural transformations. I would therefore dispute Meaghan Morris's (1990) extension of Morse that de Certeau is in general, out of touch.

[12] I should add here that I have attempted a conjunction of this type before (Buchanan, 1996b), which for reasons that I hope will become clear I am no longer completely satisfied with. This chapter should be read as a revision of that earlier attempt.

[13] It is worth noting that the ethnographic data for both of these practices of place – naming and storytelling – are taken from Pierre Mayol's account (in volume two of *The Practice of Everyday Life*) of the 'living' or 'inhabiting' practices of the people of Croix-Rousse neighbourhood in Lyons (*c* 1975–77).

Select Bibliography

De Certeau (in English)

For a complete bibliography of de Certeau's works in all languages, see Giard 1987b.

De Certeau, Michel (1964). 'Jean-Joseph Surin' in James Walsh (ed.) *Spirituality Through the Centuries. Ascetics and Mystics of the Western Church.* London: Burns and Oates, pp. 293–306.

De Certeau, Michel (1966). 'Culture and Spiritual Existence', trans. J.E. Anderson. *Concilium,* 19, pp. 3–16.

De Certeau, Michel (1970a). 'Is there a Language of Unity?', trans. Lancelot Sheppard. *Concilium,* 51, pp. 79–93.

De Certeau, Michel (1970b). 'Power Against the People', trans. Brian Darling. *New Blackfriars*, 51, pp. 338–44.

De Certeau, Michel (1971). 'How is Christianity Thinkable Today?' *Theology Digest*, 19 (4): 334–45.

De Certeau, Michel (1980a). 'On the Oppositional Practices of Everyday Life', trans. Fredric Jameson and Carl Lovitt. *Social Text,* 3: 3–43.

De Certeau, Michel (1980b). 'Writing vs. Time: History and Anthropology in the works of Lafitau', trans. James Hovde. *Yale French Studies,* 59: 37–64.

De Certeau, Michel (1983). 'The Madness of Vision', trans. Michael B. Smith. *Enclitic,* 8 (1): 24–31.

De Certeau, Michel (1984). *The Practice of Everyday Life*, trans. Steven Rendall. Berkeley: University of California Press.

De Certeau, Michel (1985a). 'Pay Attention: To Make Art', trans. Thomas DiPiero in Helen Mayer Harrison and Newton Harrison (eds),

The Lagoon Cycle. Exhibition, Herbert F. Johnson Museum of Art, Ithaca: Cornell University Press, pp. 17–23.

De Certeau, Michel (1985b). 'What We do when We Believe', trans. Richard Miller in Marshall Blonsky (ed.) *On Signs: A Semiotic Reader*. Oxford: Basil Blackwell.

De Certeau, Michel (1986). *Heterologies: Discourse on the Other*, trans. Brian Massumi. Minneapolis: University of Minnesota Press.

De Certeau, Michel (1987). 'The Gaze of Nicholas of Cusa', trans. Catherine Porter. *Diacritics,* 17 (3): 2–37.

De Certeau, Michel (1988). *The Writing of History*, trans. Tom Conley. New York: Columbia University Press.

De Certeau, Michel (1990 [1980]). *L'invention du quotidien 1. Arts de faire* (nouvelle édition). Paris: Gallimard.

De Certeau, Michel (1992). *The Mystic Fable*, trans. Michael B. Smith. Chicago: University of Chicago Press.

De Certeau, Michel (1995a). 'A Transitional Epistemology: Paul Veyne', trans. Arthur Goldhammer, in Jacques Revel and Lynn Hunt (eds) *Histories: French Constructions of the Past. Postwar French Thought, Volume 1*. New York: The New Press, pp. 310–18.

De Certeau, Michel (1995b). 'History and Mysticism', trans. Arthur Goldhammer, in Jacques Revel and Lynn Hunt (eds) *Histories: French Constructions of the Past. Postwar French Thought, Volume 1*. New York: The New Press, pp. 436–47.

De Certeau, Michel (1996a). 'History is Never Sure', trans. Michael B. Smith. *Social Semiotics,* 6 (1): 7–16.

De Certeau, Michel (1996b). 'Vocal Utopias: Glossolalias', trans. Daniel Rosenberg. *Representations,* 56: 29–47.

De Certeau, Michel (1997a). *The Capture of Speech and Other Political Writings*, trans. Tom Conley. Minneapolis: University of Minnesota Press.

De Certeau, Michel (1997b). *Culture in the Plural*, trans. Tom Conley. Minneapolis: University of Minnesota Press.

De Certeau, Michel, Luce Giard and Pierre Mayol (1998). *The Practice of Everyday Life Volume Two: Living and Cooking*, trans. Timothy J. Tomasik. Minneapolis: University of Minnesota Press.

Other Works

Ahearne, Jeremy (1995). *Michel de Certeau: Interpretation and its Other*. Cambridge: Polity.

Althusser, Louis (1971). *Lenin and Philosophy*, trans. Ben Brewster. New York: Monthly Review Press.

Asad, Talal (1973). 'Introduction' in Talal Asad (ed.) *Anthropology and the Colonial Encounter*, London: Ithaca Press, pp. 9–19.

Attridge, Derek (1996). 'Oppressive Silence: J.M. Coetzee's *Foe* and the Politics of Canonisation' in Graham Huggan and Stephen Watson (eds.) *Critical Perspectives on J.M. Coetzee*. London: Macmillan, pp. 168–90.

Augé, Marc (1995). *Non-Places: Introduction to an Anthropology of Supermodernity*, trans. John Howe. London: Verso.

Augé, Marc (1998). *A Sense for the Other: The Timeliness and Relevance of Anthropology*, trans. Amy Jacobs. Stanford: Stanford University Press.

Bakhtin, Mikhail (1981). *The Dialogic Imagination*, trans. Caryl Emerson and Michael Holquist. Austin: University of Texas Press.

Barcan, Ruth (1995). 'A Symphony of Farts: Saul Alinsky, Social Activism and Carnivalesque Transgression'. *The UTS Review,* 1 (1): 83–92.

Barthes, Roland (1972). *Mythologies*, trans. Annette Lavers. London: Paladin.

Barthes, Roland (1977). *Image, Music, Text*, trans. Stephen Heath. London: Fontana Press.

Bataille, Georges (1985). *Visions of Excess: Selected Writings 1927–1939*, trans. Allan Stoekl, with Carl R. Lovitt and Donald M. Leslie Jr. Minneapolis: University of Minnesota Press.

Benjamin, Walter (1968). *Illuminations: Essays and Reflections*, trans. Harry Zohn. New York: Schocken Books.

Benjamin, Walter (1978). *Reflections: Essays, Aphorisms, Autobiographical Writings*, trans. Edmund Jephcott. New York: Schocken Books.

Benveniste, Émile (1971). *Problems of General Linguistics*, trans. Mary Meek. Coral Gables FL: University of Miami Press.

Berman, Marshall (1988). *All That is Solid Melts into Air: The Experience of Modernity*. Harmondsworth: Penguin.

Bhabha, Homi (1995). *The Location of Culture*. London: Routledge.

Blanchot, Maurice (1993). *The Infinite Conversation*, trans. Susan Hanson. Minneapolis: University of Minnesota Press.

Bourdieu, Pierre (1988). *Homo Academicus*, trans. Peter Collier. Cambridge: Polity Press.

Brecht, Bertolt (1964). *Brecht on Theatre: The Development of an Aesthetic*, trans. and ed. John Willett. London: Methuen.

Bruno, G. (1993). *Streetwalking on a Ruined Map: Cultural Theory and the Films of Elvira Notari*. Princteon, NJ: Princeton University Press.

Buchanan, Ian (1994) 'Lefebvre and the Space of Everyday Life'. *Southern Review,* 27 (2): 127–37.

Buchanan, Ian (1995) *Heterology: Towards a Transcendental Approach to Cultural Studies*, unpublished Ph.D. dissertation, Murdoch University.

Buchanan, Ian (1996a). 'From Work to Textbook'. *Social Semiotics,* 6 (1): 147–55.

Buchanan, Ian (1996b) 'Heterophenomenology, or de Certeau's Theory of Space'. *Social Semiotics,* 6 (1): 111–32.

Buchanan, Ian (1997). 'De Certeau and Cultural Studies', *New Formations,* 31: 175–88.

Buchanan, Ian (1998a). 'Metacommentary on Utopia, or Jameson's Dialectic of Hope'. *Utopian Studies,* 9 (2): 18–29.

Buchanan, Ian (1998b). 'The Everyday is an Other'. *Antithesis,* 9: 39–56.

Buchanan, Ian (1999). 'Non-Places: Space in the Age of Supermodernity' in Ruth Barcan and Ian Buchanan (eds) *Imagining Australian Space: Cultural Studies and Spatial Inquiry.* Perth: UWA Press.

Carrard, Philippe (1992). *Poetics of the New History: French Historical Discourse from Braudel to Chartier.* Baltimore: Johns Hopkins University Press.

Chartier, Roger (1997). *On the Edge of the Cliff: History, Language and Practices,* trans. Lydia G. Cochrane. Baltimore: Johns Hopkins University Press.

Clayton, Jay (1993). *The Pleasures of Babel: Contemporary American Literature and Theory.* Oxford: Oxford University Press.

Clifford, James (1986a). 'Introduction: Partial Truths', in James Clifford and George Marcus (eds) *Writing Culture: The Poetics and Politics of Ethnography.* Berkeley: University of California Press, pp. 1–26.

Clifford, James (1986b). 'On Ethnographic Allegory' in James Clifford and George Marcus (eds) *Writing Culture: The Poetics and Politics of Ethnography.* Berkeley: University of California Press, pp. 98–121.

Clifford, James (1988). *The Predicament of Culture: Twentieth-Century Ethnography, Literature, and Art.* Cambridge, MA: Harvard University Press.

Coetzee, J.M. (1986). *Foe.* Harmondsworth: Penguin.

Colebrook, Claire (1997). *New Literary Histories: New Historicism and Contemporary Criticism.* Manchester: Manchester University Press.

Conley, Tom (1988). 'Translator's Introduction' in Michel de Certeau, *The Writing of History,* trans. Tom Conley. New York: Columbia University Press, pp. vii–xxiv.

Conley, Tom (1997). 'Afterword: The "Events" and their Erosion' in Michel de Certeau, *Capture of Speech,* trans. Tom Conley. Minnesota University Press, pp. 175–89.

Conley, Tom (2000). 'In the Savage Country', *South Atlantic Quarterly*, 99 (1).

Davis, Mike (1985). 'Urban Renaissance and the Spirit of Postmodernism', *New Left Review*, 151: 106–13.

Defoe, Daniel (1985). *Robinson Crusoe*. Harmondsworth: Penguin.

Deleuze, Gilles (1983). *Nietzsche and Philosophy*, trans. Hugh Tomlinson. London: Athlone.

Deleuze, Gilles (1988). *Foucault*, trans. Seán Hand. Minneapolis: University of Minnesota Press.

Deleuze, Gilles (1989). *Masochism: Coldness and Cruelty*, trans. Jean McNeil. New York: Zone Books.

Deleuze, Gilles (1990). *The Logic of Sense*, trans. Mark Lester. London: Athlone.

Deleuze, Gilles (1994). *Difference and Repetition,* trans. P. Patton. New York: Columbia University Press.

Deleuze, Gilles (1995). *Negotiations: 1972–1990*, trans. Martin Joughin. New York: Columbia University Press.

Deleuze, Gilles (1997). *Essays Critical and Clinical*, trans. Daniel W. Smith and Michael A. Greco. Minneapolis: University of Minnesota Press.

Deleuze, Gilles and Félix Guattari (1983). *Anti-Oedipus*, trans. Robert Hurley, Mark Seem and Helen R. Lane. Minneapolis: University of Minnesota Press.

Deleuze, Gilles and Félix Guattari (1986). *Kafka: Toward a Minor Literature*, trans. Dana Polan. Minneapolis: University of Minnesota Press.

Deleuze, Gilles and Félix Guattari (1987). *A Thousand Plateaus*, trans. Brian Massumi. Minneapolis: University of Minnesota Press.

Deleuze, Gilles and Félix Guattari (1994). *What is Philosophy?* trans. Hugh Tomlinson and Graham Burchell. New York: Columbia University Press.

Derrida, Jacques (1974). *Of Grammatology*, trans. Gayatri Chakravorty Spivak. Baltimore: Johns Hopkins University Press.

Derrida, Jacques (1978). *Writing and Difference,* trans. Alan Bass. London: Routledge & Kegan Paul.

Derrida, Jacques (1981). *Dissemination*, trans. Barbara Johnson. Chicago: Chicago University Press.

Derrida, Jacques (1984). 'Deconstruction and the Other', trans. R. Kearney, in R. Kearney (ed.) *Dialogues with Contemporary Continental Thinkers*. Manchester: Manchester University Press, pp. 107–26.

Derrida, Jacques (1994). 'The Deconstruction of Actuality', trans. J. Rée. *Radical Philosophy*, 68: 28–41.

Detienne, Marcel and Jean-Pierre Vernant (1978). *Cunning Intelligence in Greek Culture and Society*, trans. Janet Lloyd. Chicago: University of Chicago Press.

Donald, J. (1992) 'The Concept of the City and the Experience of the City' in R. Bocock and K. Thompson (eds) *Social and Cultural Forms of Modernity*. Cambridge: Polity and Open University Press, pp. 434–7.

Eagleton, Terry (1981). *Walter Benjamin, or, Towards a Revolutionary Criticism*. London: Verso.

Eco, Umberto (1983 [1980]). *The Name of the Rose*, trans. W. Weaver. London: Pan Books.

Fiske, John (1988). 'Popular Forces and the Culture of Everyday Life'. *Southern Review,* 21 (3): 288–306.

Fiske, John (1989). *Understanding Popular Culture*. Boston: Unwin Hyman.

Foucault, Michel (1970). *The Order of Things*, trans. A. Sheridan-Smith. London: Tavistock.

Foucault, Michel (1973). *The Birth of the Clinic*, trans. A.M. Sheridan. London: Tavistock.

Foucault, Michel (1978). *The History of Sexuality: An Introduction*, trans. Robert Hurley. Harmondsworth: Penguin.

Foucault, Michel (1979). *Discipline and Punish: The Birth of the Prison*, trans. A. Sheridan. Harmondsworth: Peregrine.

Foucault, Michel (1987). *The Thought from the Outside*, trans. Brian Massumi. New York: Zone Books.

Foucault, Michel (1997). *Ethics: The Essential Works 1*, trans. Robert Hurley et al. New York: The New Press.

Freud, Sigmund (1984). *On Metapsychology*, trans. James Strachey. Harmondsworth: Penguin Freud Library.

Frow, John (1991). 'Michel de Certeau and the Practice of Representation'. *Cultural Studies,* 5 (1): 52–60.

Frow, John (1992). 'The Concept of the Popular'. *New Formations,* 18: 25–38.

Geertz, Clifford (1973). *The Interpretation of Cultures*. New York: Basic Books.

Geertz, Clifford (1983). *Local Knowledge*. New York: Basic Books.

Geertz, Clifford (1995). 'Disciplines'. *Raritan,* 14: 65–102.

Geffré, Claude (ed.) (1991). *Michel de Certeau ou la Différence Chrétienne*. Paris: Les Éditions du Cerf.

Geldof, Koenraad (1997). 'Authority, Reading, Reflexivity: Pierre Bourdieu and the Aesthetic Judgement of Kant'. *Diacritics,* 27 (1): 20–43.

Giard, Luce (ed.) (1987a). *Michel de Certeau*. Paris: Éditions du Centre Pompidou.

Giard, Luce (1987b). 'Biobibliographie' in Luce Giard (ed.) *Michel de Certeau*. Paris: Éditions du Centre Pompidou, pp. 245–53.

Giard, Luce (ed.) (1988). *Le Voyage Mystique Michel de Certeau*. (a special double issue of *Recherches de Science Religieuse,* 76 (2/3): 161–457). Paris: Les Éditions du Cerf.

Giard, Luce (1990). 'Histoire d'une Recherche' introduction to Michel de Certeau *L'invention du Quotidien 1.: Arts de Faire*. Paris: Gallimard, pp. i–xxx.

Giard, Luce (1991a). 'Michel de Certeau's Heterology and the New World'. *Representations,* 33: 212–26.

Giard, Luce (1991b). 'Mystique et politique, ou l'institution comme objet second' in Luce Giard and Pierre-Jean Labarrière (eds) *Histoire, Mystique et Politique Michel de Certeau*. Grenoble: Editions Jérôme Millon, pp. 9–56.

Giard, Luce (1991c). 'Epilogue: Michel de Certeau's Heterology and the New World', trans. K. Streip. *Representations,* 33: 212–21.

Giard, Luce (1997a). 'How Tomorrow is Already Being Born' in Michel de Certeau, *The Capture of Speech and Other Political Writings*. Minneapolis: University of Minnesota Press, pp. vii–xix.

Giard, Luce (1997b). 'Opening the Possible' in Michel de Certeau, *Culture in the Plural*. Minneapolis: University of Minnesota Press, pp. ix–xv.

Giard, Luce (1998a). 'History of a Research Project', in Michel de Certeau, Luce Giard and Pierre Mayol, *The Practice of Everyday Life Volume Two: Living and Cooking*. Minneapolis: University of Minnesota Press, pp. xiii–xxxiii.

Giard, Luce (1998b). 'Times and Places', in Michel de Certeau, Luce Giard and Pierre Mayol, *The Practice of Everyday Life Volume Two: Living and Cooking*. Minneapolis: University of Minnesota Press, pp. xxxv–xlv.

Gregory, Derek (1994). *Geographical Imaginations*. Oxford: Blackwell.

Greimas, Algirdas Julien (1987). *On Meaning: Selected Writings in Semiotics Theory*, trans. Paul J. Perron and Frank H. Collins. Minneapolis: University of Minnesota Press.

Haraway, Donna J. (1991). *Simians, Cyborgs, and Women: The Reinvention of Nature*. London: Routledge.

Hartog, François (1987). 'L'écriture du voyage', in Luce Giard (ed.) *Michel de Certeau*. Paris: Éditions du Centre Pompidou, pp. 123–32.

Harvey, David (1996). *Justice, Nature and the Geography of Difference*. Oxford: Blackwell.

Heidegger, Martin (1962). *Being and Time*, trans. J. Macquarrie and E. Robinson. Oxford: Blackwell.

Jacobs, Jane (1961). *The Death and Life of Great American Cities*. Harmondsworth: Penguin.

Jameson, Fredric (1961). *Sartre: The Origins of a Style*. New York: Columbia University Press.

Jameson, Fredric (1972). *The Prison-House of Language: A Critical Account of Structuralism and Russian Formalism*. Princeton: Princeton University Press.

Jameson, Fredric (1981). *The Political Unconscious: Narrative as Socially Symbolic Act*. London: Routledge.

Jameson, Fredric (1987). 'Foreword' in Algirdas Julien Greimas, *On Meaning: Selected Writings in Semiotics Theory*, trans. Paul J. Perron and Frank H. Collins. Minneapolis: University of Minnesota Press.

Jameson, Fredric (1988a). *The Ideologies of Theory: Essays 1971– 1986. Volume 1: Situations of Theory*. Minneapolis: University of Minnesota Press.

Jameson, Fredric (1988b). *The Ideologies of Theory: Essays 1971– 1986. Volume 2: Syntax of History*. Minneapolis: University of Minnesota Press.

Jameson, Fredric (1990). *Late Marxism: Adorno, or, The Persistence of the Dialectic*. London: Verso.

Jameson, Fredric (1991). *Postmodernism, or, the Cultural Logic of Late Capitalism*. Durham: Duke University Press.

Jameson, Fredric (1992a). *Signatures of the Visible*. London: Routledge.

Jameson, Fredric (1992b). *The Geopolitical Aesthetic: Cinema and Space in the World System*. London: BFI Publishing.

Jameson, Fredric (1994). *The Seeds of Time*. New York: Columbia University Press.

Jameson, Fredric (1997). 'Marxism and Dualism in Deleuze'. *South Atlantic Quarterly,* 96 (3): 393–416.

Jameson, Fredric (1998). *The Cultural Turn: Selected Writings on the Postmodern, 1983–1998.* London: Verso.

Jameson, Fredric (1999). 'The Theoretical Hesitation: Benjamin's Sociological Predecessor'. *Critical Inquiry,* 25 (2): 267–88.

Jenkins, Henry (1992). *Textual Poachers: Television Fans and Participatory Culture.* London: Routledge.

Jullien, François (1995). *The Propensity of Things: Toward a History of Efficacy in China,* trans. Janet Lloyd. New York: Zone Books.

Lacan, Jacques (1977). *Écrits: A Selection,* trans. Alan Sheridan. New York: W.W. Norton.

Lacan, Jacques (1979). *The Four Fundamental Concepts of Psycho-Analysis,* trans. Alan Sheridan. Harmondsworth: Penguin.

Langbauer, Laurie (1999). *Novels of Everyday Life: The Series in English Fiction, 1850–1930.* Ithaca: Cornell University Press.

Le Brun, Jacques (1988). 'Le Secret d'un Travail', in Luce Giard (ed.) *Le Voyage Mystique Michel de Certeau.* Paris: Les Éditions du Cerf, pp. 77–91.

Le Goff, Jacques (1992). *History and Memory,* trans. Steven Rendall and Elizabeth Claman. New York: Columbia University Press.

Levinas, Emmanuel (1969). *Totality and Infinity: An Essay on Exteriority,* trans. Alphonso Lingis. Pittsburgh: Duquesne University Press.

Levinas, Emmanuel (1987). *Time and the Other and Additional Essays,* trans. R. Cohen. Pittsburgh: Duquesne University Press.

Lynch, Kevin (1960). *The Image of the City.* Cambridge, MA: MIT Press.

Lyotard, Jean-François (1984). *The Postmodern Condition: A Report on Knowledge,* trans. Geoff Bennington and Brian Massumi. Minneapolis: University of Minnesota Press.

Lyotard, Jean-François (1988). *The Differend: Phrases in Dispute,* trans. Georges Van Den Abbeele. Manchester: Manchester University Press.

Lyotard, Jean-François (1993). *Libidinal Economy*, trans. Iain Hamilton Grant. London: Athlone.

Lyotard, Jean-François and Jean-Loup Thébaud (1985). *Just Gaming,* trans. Wlad Godzich. Manchester: Manchester University Press.

Merleau-Ponty, Maurice (1962). *Phenomenology of Perception,* trans. Colin Smith. London: Routledge & Kegan Paul.

Moignt, Joseph (1996). 'Traveller of Culture: Michel de Certeau', in Graham Ward (ed.) *Michel de Certeau SJ.* Edinburgh: English Dominicans, pp. 479–84.

Morris, Meaghan (1990). 'Banality in Cultural Studies', in Patricia Mellancamp (ed.) *The Logics of Television: Essays in Cultural Criticism.* Bloomington and Indianapolis: Indiana University Press, pp. 14–43.

Morse, Margaret (1990). 'An Ontology of Everyday Distraction: The Freeway, the Mall, and Television', in Patricia Mellencamp (ed.) *The Logics of Television: Essays in Cultural Criticism.* Bloomington and Indianapolis: Indiana University Press, pp. 193–221.

Norris, Christopher (1993). *The Truth About Postmodernism.* Oxford: Blackwell.

Norris, Christopher (1994). *Truth and the Ethics of Criticism.* Manchester: Manchester University Press.

Novick, P. (1988). *That Noble Dream: The 'Objectivity Question' and the American Historical Profession.* Cambridge: Cambridge University Press.

Pickering, Jean and Suzanne Kehde (1998). 'Reading de Certeau through Mahasweta Devi – and Vice Versa'. *Narrative,* 6 (3): 341–51.

Quine, W.V. and J.S. Ullian (1970). *The Web of Belief.* New York: Random House.

Read, Alan (1993). *Theatre and Everyday Life: An Ethics of Performance.* London: Routledge.

Ricoeur, Paul (1970). *Freud and Philosophy: An Essay on Interpretation*, trans. Denis Savage. New Haven: Yale University Press.

Ricoeur, Paul (1988). *Time and Narrative: Volume 3*, trans. Kathleen Blamey and David Pellauer. Chicago: Chicago University Press.

Rigby, Brian (1991). *Popular Culture in Modern France: A Study of Cultural Discourse*. London: Routledge.

Rosello, Mireille (1994). 'The Screener's Maps: Michel de Certeau's *"Wandersmanner"* and Paul Auster's Hypertextual Detective' in George P. Landow (ed.) *Hyper/Text/Theory*. Baltimore: Johns Hopkins University Press.

Ross, Kristin (1997). 'The Sociologist and the Priest'. *Sites,* 1 (1): 17–30.

Ruddick, Susan (1990). 'Heterotopias of the Homeless: Strategies and Tactics of Placemaking in Los Angeles'. *Strategies,* 3: 184–201.

Said, Edward (1991) *Orientalism: Western Conceptions of the Orient.* Harmondsworth: Penguin.

Said, Edward (1993). *Culture and Imperialism.* London: Chatto and Windus.

Scott, Joan (1991). 'Women's History', in Peter Burke (ed.) *New Perspectives on Historical Writing*. Cambridge: Polity, pp. 42–66.

Silverstone, Roger (1989). 'Let us then Return to the Murmuring of Everyday Practices: A Note on Michel de Certeau, Television and Everyday Life'. *Theory, Culture and Society,* 6: 77–94.

Soja, Edward (1989). *Postmodern Geographies: The Reassertion of Space in Critical Theory*. London: Verso.

Soja, Edward (1996). *Thirdspace: Journeys to Los Angeles and Other Real-and-Imagined Places*. Oxford: Blackwell.

Terdiman, Richard (1992). 'The Response of the Other'. *Diacritics,* 22 (2): 2–10.

Thrift, Nigel (1996). *Spatial Formations.* London: Sage.

Todorov, Tzvetan (1973). *The Fantastic: A Structural Approach to a Literary Genre*, trans. Richard Howard. Ithaca: Cornell University Press.

Tuan, Yi-Fu (1977). *Space and Place: The Perspective of Experience.* Minneapolis: University of Minnesota Press.

Ward, Graham (ed.) (1996). *Michel de Certeau SJ* (special issue of *New Blackfriars,* 77 (909): 478–528). Edinburgh: English Dominicans.

Weber, Max. (1963). *The Sociology of Religion*, trans. Ephraim Fischoff. Boston: Beacon Press.

White, Hayden. (1973). *Metahistory: The Historical Imagination in Nineteenth Century Europe*, Baltimore: Johns Hopkins University Press.

White, Hayden. (1978). *Tropics of Discourse: Essays in Cultural Criticism*, Baltimore: Johns Hopkins University Press.

White, Hayden. (1987). *The Content of the Form: Narrative Discourse and Historical Representation*, Baltimore: Johns Hopkins University Press.

Yúdice, George (1988). 'Marginality and the Ethics of Survival' in Andrew Ross (ed.) *Universal Abandon? The Politics of Postmodernism.* Minneapolis: University of Minnesota Press.

Index